TO SEE DIFFERENTLY

SUSAN TROUT'S
OTHER WORKS INCLUDE:

ATTITUDINAL HEALING PRINCIPLES: A CARD SET
(Three Roses Press: Alexandria, VA, 1990)

BORN TO SERVE: THE EVOLUTION OF THE SOUL
THROUGH SERVICE
(Three Roses Press: Alexandria, VA, 1997)

TO SEE DIFFERENTLY

Personal Growth and Being of Service
Through Attitudinal Healing

Susan S. Trout, Ph.D.

Three Roses Press
Alexandria, VA

Although the personal stories in this book are true, names have been changed to honor the privacy of those involved.

Throughout this book, masculine pronouns are used as universal markers of person. This has been done in the interest of ease of reading. Please join in a loving acceptance of the limitations of our language.

Printings: 1990, 1992, 1996

Three Roses Press
P.O. Box 19222
Alexandria, VA 22320

ISBN: 0-9625386-0-4 (pbk)
Library of Congress Catalog Card Number: 89-52112

Cover design by Rosemary Moak
Text design by Cleveland Wheat

Printed in the United States of America

To my parents, George and Ruth Struve,
to my brother, John, and to my sisters,
Mary and Betty

*t he last of the human freedoms
... to choose one's attitude in
any given set of circumstances,
to choose one's way.*

Viktor E. Frankl

CONTENTS

ACKNOWLEDGEMENTS

The completion of this book is clearly the result of many loving hands and hearts. From the time that the idea for this book was suggested to me by Molly Whitehouse four years ago to the time I finally wrote it this year, the universe has clearly supported its creation and publication. I am profoundly grateful to:

The Board of Directors, staff, facilitators, families, workshop and support program participants at the Institute for Attitudinal Studies and to my private practice clients for generously sharing their healing process with me during the past ten years and for helping me understand the relationship between personal growth and being of service to others.

The Center for Attitudinal Healing in Tiburon, California, for being the spark that lit the light for the development of attitudinal healing.

Peggy Tabor Millin, for her extraordinary competence in editing, for her unconditional high regard and understanding of the philosophy contained in this book and for our harmonious working relationship as a writer-editor team.

Rosemary Moak, for her gentle and loving gift of creating a book cover design which reflects and honors the healing process and serving others.

13

Marilyn Wood, for her expert care in handling the various publishing needs of the book.

Cleveland Wheat, for lovingly and capably preparing the manuscript for printing and binding.

Christian Skeem, for his loving gift of a computer on which to write the book.

Judith Skutch Whitson, for generously opening many doors of opportunity to me ten years ago; the gifts of these opportunities are still revealing themselves.

Sharon Browne, for first teaching me the true meaning and essence of a supportive relationship.

The book's forty-five manuscript readers, for generously sharing their thoughtful responses and suggestions.

And, the extraordinary people who throughout the years have inspired me to move through and beyond the belief in my limited self, and who extended their love and support to me during the intense years of my own healing process.

Susan S. Trout
December, 1989

THE BOOK AS
A COMPANION

IN THE SEARCH FOR WHOLENESS THERE IS NO ONE WAY. THERE IS ONLY YOUR WAY. THIS BOOK IS YOURS TO HAVE AS FRIEND AND SUPPORTER, AS GUIDE AND MENTOR, TO USE AS CREATIVELY AS SERVES YOUR NEEDS.

WHAT IS THE BOOK'S PURPOSE?

The purpose of this book is to guide those who wish to heal their attitudes about themselves, relationships, events and situations and feel a calling to serve others as a natural extension of that healing.

This is a practical book. What you learn can be immediately applied in your personal life, in relationships with family and friends, in work relationships and in life circumstances. What you learn can also be used as a way of supporting another person's healing process.

The book is not about learning how to control or change outer events and people. Rather, it is about healing your mind and changing your perceptions of these events and people.

WHO IS THE BOOK FOR?

You will find this book useful if you feel comfortable with the philosophical premises of attitudinal healing as described in Chapter One and have a desire to experience your relationships in a way that serves your own and another's healing.

Attitudinal healing is relevant for anyone – parent, teacher, carpet cleaner, helping professional, government worker, business person, taxi cab driver or graduate student. There are no prerequisites to working with this book other than an open mind, a willing heart and a desire to live a more peaceful life. A desire to be of direct service to others is not a prerequisite. If you feel no calling to be of direct service at this time, simply focus on the sections in the book on healing your personal attitudes.

Although attitudinal healing has its philosophical basis in the metaphysical teachings of *A Course in Miracles,* you do not have to be a student of the *Course* to practice attitudinal healing or to benefit from this book.

HOW IS THE BOOK ORGANIZED?

There are two parts to this book. Part One discusses the philosophical premises of attitudinal healing, the nature of the healing process, the levels and attributes of being of service and the facilitator guidelines for use in supporting others. I recommend that you first read the book through for a general understanding of the concepts and without doing the exercises. As you reread the book and work with the principles in Part Two, it will be helpful to periodically review Part One. This will help maintain the continuity of your inner process and reaffirm the philosophical context in which you are studying and applying the principles and guidelines.

Part Two addresses the twelve principles. With each principle, you are guided through the following sequence:

Step 1: The Principle's Message

This section begins with a list of the ten major tenets of the principle. These tenets define the principle and describe its major characteristics. The tenets provide you with the philosophical foundation behind the principle. All exercises and suggestions for each principle are an expression of these tenets in action. The tenets are followed by a discussion of important aspects of the principle and sharing of relevant personal anecdotes.

Step 2: What Is My Attitude?

You are asked seven questions about your current attitudes that relate to a specific principle. You may choose to write your responses in a journal or you may contemplate them. The purpose of these questions is to increase your awareness of both the meaning of the principle and its practical application in your daily life.

Step 3: Practicing the Principle

Several exercises are provided to facilitate your personal healing process with each principle.   These exercises support your understanding and application of the principle in your life. You may want to select those exercises that particularly speak to your process or you may want to do all of them. Keeping a journal will assist your process. Rereading a journal is one way to observe your growth. You may want to audiotape the visualization exercises that require closed eyes or an inward focus. The time you decide to spend with the exercises will depend on what best serves you and your process.

Step 4: Have I Healed My Attitude?

Seven follow-up questions serve to measure your progress with a principle. These thought-provoking questions give you feedback regarding any shifts in your attitude. You may want to journal your responses and compare them with the inventory you took before working with the principle.

Step 5: Applying the Principle in Service

This section reinforces the principle's meaning and explains how it can be practically applied when supporting someone. This section can be useful even if you are not involved in direct service to another. The suggestions are relevant for use in such roles as spouse, parent, sibling, teacher, student and friend.

Step 6: How Am I Doing?

This inventory of self-evaluation questions increases your awareness of the quality and progress of your facility in serving others. You will find it helpful to either journal or contemplate your responses.

HOW MUCH TIME SHOULD I SPEND WITH EACH PRINCIPLE?

There are no time limits for working with each principle. Although I recommend spending a month on each principle, I strongly encourage you to select your pacing according to your unique needs and nature. Allow the book to support and empower you by adapting it to your individual process. It is important to allow sufficient time to absorb and apply what you are learning so that you have an experience of embodying the essence of the principle.

DO I NEED TO DO THE PRINCIPLES IN ORDER?

In general, I suggest that you work with the principles in the order they are given to ensure continuity of your process. The work on future principles is often a continuation of previous ones or carries the reader to the next level of understanding.

However, you may feel guided not to do the principles in the order they are given, choosing instead to work with a principle that specifically addresses your needs at a particular time. The principles are presented in such a way that sufficient value can be gained by selecting and working with a principle out of order. Again, adapt the book to respond to your needs.

WHAT KINDS OF EXERCISES ARE IN THE BOOK?

There are several psychological disciplines and spiritual traditions that are particularly compatible with attitudinal healing. These include gestalt, psychosynthesis, dream psychology, depth psychology, meditation and various Eastern philosophies. Tools and techniques which seem to effectively support the process of attitudinal healing are dreamwork, journaling, impromptu drawing, meditation, visualization, music, guided imagery, affirmations and effective communication and listening skills. When appropriate these traditions and techniques are integrated into the book's discussion of the meaning and application of the various principles and into the suggested exercises.

WHAT ARE THE LEVELS OF INVOLVEMENT WITH THE BOOK?

You can decide to use this book with a varying degree of involvement.

1. Read quickly through the book to gain an overview of its contents and return to the book when ready to do deeper work.

2. Work only with the personal growth sections.

3. Select only those exercises which serve your needs.

4. Follow the book in its entirety, including the personal growth sections and the sections on serving others.

WHAT DOES IT MEAN TO FACILITATE AND TO BE A FACILITATOR IN THE CONTEXT OF THIS BOOK?

The terms *facilitate* and *facilitator* are used to describe the unique nature of the supportive process within the context of attitudinal healing. A facilitator is any person who supports another person's process by creating a safe environment, by honoring the healing process and by staying on purpose with the principles and the facilitator guidelines. The role of the facilitator is to create an atmosphere in which a person can find his own answers with greater ease than he could on his own. A facilitator in attitudinal healing views service both as a state of mind and as love in action. Chapter Four explains both the facilitating process and the attitude of the facilitator.

One can facilitate another within both an informal and formal structure, such as having a private session with someone, taking a walk together, meeting for lunch or speaking on the telephone. It is important to remember that facilitators within the context of this book do not refer to professionally trained individuals. The book uses the term facilitator to refer to people supporting people as a *natural* part of life. The act of facilitating is not separated from ordinary living; it is a dynamic part of it.

WHAT SETTINGS WOULD FACILITATE USE OF THE BOOK?

This book can be used alone by an individual, with another person or in small groups. It can also be used in conjunction with or as a supplement to counseling or therapy.

Joining with someone in working with the book can be particularly useful and supportive. Two people can serve as "buddies" for one another, facilitating and supporting each other's process. Buddies can share their responses to the inventory questions and their experiences with the various exercises. They might also lead one another through the exercises.

The book can also be effectively used in a group setting. Once group members have read through the book and gained an appreciation of its content and structure, they can decide how to proceed with each principle. One group member might facilitate a given chapter. The principle's message could be discussed along with responses to the inventory questions. Exercises can be selected and used which reflect the interests and needs of the group.

The following is a suggested outline for group study. This outline assumes that the members have read the chapter and have done some independent work with the inventory questions prior to the group meeting.

Opening meditation or centering

Discussion of the principle's tenets and meaning

Sharing of feelings and insights experienced during the exercises

Selection of an exercise to do as a group

Sharing of individual experiences of that exercise

Discussion of how the principle relates to serving others

Sharing of experiences in supporting others within the context of the principle

Closing meditation or exercise

THE BOOK AS A COMPANION 21

HOW DO I USE A JOURNAL WITH THE BOOK?

The chapter sections WHAT IS MY ATTITUDE?, PRACTICING THE PRINCIPLE, HAVE I HEALED MY ATTITUDE? and HOW AM I DOING? are all introduced with the suggestion that you write your responses in a journal. You can also keep a log of your dreams in the journal and add various drawings, affirmations, sayings or pictures which reinforce your healing process and serve to acknowledge your insights and progress.

Journaling will assist you in observing the process and progress of your personal growth. As you proceed, you may want to reread your earlier responses to a principle's inventory questions and note whether or not you would now answer them differently.

If journaling presents an obstacle for you, you may simply contemplate the questions. You still may wish to write key words to help you recall your thoughts later or draw pictures of your experiences of visualizations. Use whatever techniques feel comfortable to you. You may find as the healing process unfolds, that journaling ceases to be an obstacle and becomes a powerful tool.

HOW SHALL I VIEW MY PROCESS WHILE WORKING WITH THE PRINCIPLES?

Be gentle with yourself as you proceed through the book and work with the principles. If you begin to experience fear and discomfort, you may want to share these feelings with a trusted friend or perhaps the buddy who is sharing your work with the book. The book can be used as an adjunct to therapy and may also lead you to the realization that individual therapy might be helpful at this time in your life. Chapter Three provides you with some understanding and guidance regarding the nature of your psyche and the healing process.

INTRODUCTION

In the early 1970's, I became aware of a dramatic philosophical shift that was occurring throughout the world. I was especially cognizant of the shift taking place in California, where I was living at the time. Suddenly there were numerous conferences, workshops and courses available that focused on personal growth and new approaches to health, education and science.

We had just moved out of the social activism of the 1960's as a way to bring about change in our world and had openly embarked on another approach, that of changing from the inside out. Words such as transformation, holistic health, humanistic psychology, mind-body connection, spirituality and personal growth peppered the conversations of my colleagues and friends and began to appear in the media. There was a feeling of expectancy as people began to examine and take responsibility for the lack of emotional and spiritual well-being in their lives. Something new and wonderful seemed to be on the way that would carry us safely out of our state of inner turmoil and confusion. The message was that there was another way to live in this world.

A new paradigm for delivering physical and mental health care actively began at this point. Today you can witness this phenomenon by the number of scientists, physicians, psychologists, teachers and others who, out of their own personal transformation, are making significant contributions towards the healing of others. Elisabeth Kübler-Ross, Judith Skutch Whitson, Ira Progoff, Norman Cousins and Stephen Levine are just a few of the thousands who have made an impact in this way.

Techniques for facilitating this personal transformation began to emerge and flower during the 1970's. These included such programs as *est*, Lifespring and Parent Effectiveness Training, and such approaches as psychosynthesis, gestalt, intensive journaling, acupuncture, meditation, visualization, music and guided imagery and, of course, attitudinal healing.

My own personal and emotional crisis occurred at this same time. Out of my despair, I began an inner journey for my own healing. And like many others who have embarked on this journey, I soon discovered that to change from the inside out was to have the effect of changing the world.

During my healing process, I explored many techniques, approaches and philosophies. The one which provided a framework best suited to my own needs was *A Course in Miracles*.[1] *A Course in Miracles* is a metaphysical teaching which focuses on the healing of the mind. Often referred to as spiritual psychotherapy, it challenges us to see ourselves and the events in the world differently. The *Course* was scribed soon after psychologists William Thetford and Helen Schucman agreed that "there must be a better way" to view their relationship to one another and to their colleagues. At the time Helen began to scribe the *Course*, she and Bill had a history of conflict between them and within the university department where they worked. (For a thorough overview of the history of how the *Course* came into being, the reader is referred to Kenneth Wapnick's book *Absence from Felicity* or the book *Journey Without Distance* by Robert Skutch.[2])

The *Course* deals solely with the healing of the mind and does not make any suggestions as to what form this might take. The student is not advised to be a vegetarian, to be rolfed, to listen to certain music or to change his behavior in any way. Changing behavior without addressing the conditions that created that behavior does not result in healing the mind. The content of the *Course* is designed to refocus the mind, shifting its perception from wrongmindedness to rightmindedness, the latter being led by spirit and the former by the ego.

I have found the *Course* extremely practical in that through teaching how to access one's own inner guidance, it teaches how to be in this world and be happy. Always one is asked to look within for inner guidance so that the highest good for everyone can be served in any situation. This necessitates a prayerful attitude and a willingness to allow the removal of the obstacles to hearing this guidance. The student always has the choice of whether or not to follow the guidance; however, the discovery is quickly made that only through following the guidance can happiness be attained.

The principles of attitudinal healing were selected from the *Course* by psychiatrist Jerry Jampolsky. He applied these universal principles in his work with children with life-threatening illnesses when, in 1976, he and others established the first Center for Attitudinal Healing in Tiburon, California. The term "attitudinal healing" came to Judith Skutch Whitson during a meditation in which she and Jerry were seeking inner guidance. Judith serves as President of the Foundation for Inner Peace which publishes and disseminates the *Course*. Today she continues that effort, supervising the translation of the *Course* into fourteen languages and distributing it around the world.

Attitudinal healing is seen as one form in which the *Course* can be expressed. It focuses on the key universal concepts which are applicable for people of many psychological and spiritual traditions. It is not necessary to be a student of the *Course* to practice attitudinal healing. It is only necessary to be willing to see differently and to want to look within for the peace and equanimity that would bring one a sense of emotional and spiritual well-being.

In 1980, I assisted in the founding of the Washington Center for Attitudinal Healing in Washington, D.C., which, in 1990, became the Institute for Attitudinal Studies. The Institute offers support groups, facilitation and conflict resolution services, study groups, courses and workshops that support the emotional and spiritual well-being of people of all ages and in all varieties of life circumstances. In addition, adults and high school students can receive training at the Institute in facilitation and conflict resolution. Other trainings are offered in leadership, organizational design, team building, group process and conflict resolution. Volunteer facilitators come from all walks of life and work at the Institute as their way of serving the community and actively working on their own healing. All facilitators must complete a six-month training course.

Attitudinal healing is about working on one's own healing process and being of service to others. It is a way of life; one can practice attitudinal healing anytime, anywhere and with anyone. It is about healing the mind so that one can live in this world with a sense of peace within and in relationships. It is about understanding the dynamics of the human psyche at both its conscious and unconscious levels. Above all, it is a way to care for one's emotional and spiritual well-being.

This book is an extension of my personal healing and an expression of the work at our Institute. Thousands of people caught in a myriad of stressful and troubled life circumstances have attended support programs, workshops and trainings or have sought Institute support in other ways. The healing experiences of these people provide the proof of the validity of the attitudinal healing principles. It is important for both the Institute and the individual to continually examine whether use of the principles affects the quality of life and relationships, enhances and increases feelings of inner peace or heals painful attitudes. It is, after all, only through the application of a teaching that the truth of the teaching can be tested.

There are many paths one can take in caring for his emotional and spiritual well-being. In *The Teachings of Don Juan,* Carlos Casteneda requests Don Juan's advice on how to choose the path to follow. Don Juan replies:

> Anything is one of a million paths. Therefore you must always keep in mind that a path is only a path. If you feel you should not follow it, you must not stay with it under any conditions. To have such clarity you must lead a disciplined life.

Don Juan suggests asking:

> Does this path have heart? If it does, the path is good; if it doesn't, it is of no use. Both paths lead nowhere; but one has heart, the other doesn't. One makes for a joyful journey; as long as you follow it, you are one with it. The other will make you curse your life. One makes you strong; the other weakens you.[3]

Attitudinal healing is one such path. For me and for many others, it is a path with heart. If it beckons you, I invite you to use it to walk through your own hurt and suffering. Attitudinal healing is essentially a path to inner peace, a journey of joy, a way to see differently.

PART ONE

Attitudinal Healing

Chapter One

PHILOSOPHICAL
FOUNDATIONS

Attitudinal healing is the ongoing process of healing the mind so that we can experience inner peace. This entails choosing a perception of the world that mirrors the inner state we want to create. To make this choice, we must address the condition of our minds.

Few people today understand how their mind works, how to keep it healthy or how to support the health and well-being of the minds of others. We are taught to read and write, to open a checking account and to drive a car. We are *not* taught to confront our conflicts, to lovingly relate to others and to feel safe in a seemingly unsafe world.

We are not taught how to maintain and care for that most precious, invisible part of ourselves that we experience but do not see – the mind. We know more about how to abuse our mind than how to keep it healthy. How much easier it is to maintain the health of our mind than it is to repair it after it has been damaged or fragmented.

In 1974, I was faced with the consequences of neglect and abuse of my own mind. I was a mass of negativity, rage and grief. This state of mind was the result of years of ignoring my emotional and spiritual needs. Unshed tears, undelivered communications, suppressed anger and fear, failure to experience meaning and purpose, estranged personal relationships and a "me against them" attitude prevailed in my life. I sought solace and comfort in the externals of life, especially in achievement, work, substances and relationships. I felt betrayed by others, by God and by myself. I did not know what to do about my unhealed mental state, particularly when I reached a place I called the "abyss of despair."

I recall waking up the morning of my thirty-fifth birthday with a startling thought, "Well, Susan, if you don't get your life together this lifetime, you'll just have to come back and do it again." I got dressed and went to work.

At that time I was a professor and chairperson of a university medical center department for neurological learning and behavior problems in children and adults. I had noticed that one of the faculty members with whom I worked had seemed to be more contented of late. It was into her office I walked that morning and announced, "I refuse to be miserable anymore." In that instant I knew I had made a choice to be healed and that I was going to take the necessary steps to bring it about.

One Sunday afternoon soon after this, my former husband against whom I held what I believed to be an absolutely justifiable and unforgivable grievance, came to visit me. He brought with him a black binder on whose pages were written such words as forgiveness, guiltlessness, innocence, joining and inner peace. He said these pages were from a then unpublished book called *A Course in Miracles.* He insisted I keep the binder, saying the *Course* had helped him and maybe it would help me.

I begrudgingly took the book and when he left, I put it in the darkest corner of my darkest closet in a room whose door I rarely opened.

Some weeks later, still in a bitter, resentful, unforgiving and justified state of mind, I was getting something from that closet and came upon the binder again.

For some reason, I opened it. This time my eyes fell upon the words "How willing are you to forgive your brother? How much do you desire peace instead of endless strife and misery and pain? These questions are the same, in different form. Forgiveness is your peace. . ."[1] Only because the book specifically addressed the issue of resentment and promised a way to be healed of emotional pain, did I take it out of the closet and begin to read it.

Once I made the commitment to my own healing, it was as though I had opened a door through which flowed all the structure, guidance and content that I, in particular, needed. I experienced what W. H. Murray wrote:

> Until one is committed
> there is hesitancy, the chance to draw back,
> always ineffectiveness.
> Concerning all acts of initiative (and creation),
> there is one elementary truth,
> the ignorance of which kills countless ideas
> and splendid plans:

that the moment one definitely commits oneself,
then Providence moves too.
All sorts of things occur to help one
that would never otherwise have occurred.
A whole stream of events issues from the decision,
raising in one's favour all manner
of unforeseen incidents and meetings
and material assistance,
which no man could have dreamt
would have come his way.

I have learned a deep respect
for one of Goethe's couplets:
"Whatever you can do, or dream you can, begin it.
Boldness has genius, power, and magic in it."[2]

My healing journey began with being introduced to a myriad of techniques and approaches. I read books and took trainings and workshops in dream psychology, meditation, gestalt psychology, mysticism, psychosynthesis, depth psychology, journaling, Eastern traditions and metaphysics. I attended every holistic health conference held on the West Coast between 1974 and 1979. Seen and unseen helpers entered my life and guided me with wisdom and care. Loving hands were extended to me, hands that brought me out of the quicksand onto dry land.

I began to observe a relationship between my personal healing and the quality and creativity of my professional work. As I began to heal emotionally and study psychological and spiritual disciplines, I began to share this healing with others. There was a direct correlation between the changes in my inner life and what was reflected in my outer life. I saw that a natural expression of one's own healing is the desire to share it with others. There is truth in the adage that says to keep what you know as truth you must continually give it away to others. True healing, by its nature, wants to be shared.

The greatest gift of this intense five-year period was the awareness that I did not have to live a life of emotional pain. For the first time, I saw the possibility of experiencing peace of mind while on this earth.

Nothing is learned in isolation. While I was taking classes and reading books and studying the *Course*, I was unconsciously integrating, sifting and reintegrating the material. I realized that there is a core of Truth that underlies all great teachings, whether acknowledged or not. It is this core, in the form of basic assumptions about the structure of the universe and our relationship to it, that became the sieve through which I strained new information. These same assumptions are at the heart of the *Course* and of attitudinal healing.

1. There is a Divine Source, an Eternal, a Higher Power, a God, Goddess, All That Is. Each of us is part of this Source like a droplet of ocean water while not being the ocean is part of the ocean.

2. When we set our personality or ego selves aside, we can hear an Inner Voice which speaks to us from this Source. When we follow the guidance of this Inner Voice, the highest good is always said or done in any situation.

3. We have created obstacles in our minds that distort, block or interfere with our hearing that Voice. These obstacles take the form of guilt, fear, anger, resentment, low self-worth, competition, condemnation, denial, rejection and any other judgements of self or others.

4. There are two emotions: love and fear. All other feelings are merely forms of one of these. Love is our natural state, our connection with the Source; fear is the creation of obstacles to avoid accepting our connection.

5. Forgiveness is the undoing of these obstacles. It is releasing the past so that neither past nor future expectations are brought into the present moment. Forgiveness is acknowledging the presence of the Divine in each individual, regardless of what he has done or said. To experience forgiveness, one need do nothing except perceive the person in the shared identity of Divinity.

6. All healing is of the mind. All that we experience in our lives and in our bodies is a reflection of the healed or unhealed mind.

7. Minds are joined. Our thoughts create our experience and connect with all other minds. We are constantly creating through this means. Through conscious choice we can decide to create only those experiences which promote peace.

8. The basic problem in our lives is that we have forgotten our Oneness with the Divine Source. The basic solution is remembering our true identity. All situations of conflict are a form of forgetting this identity. Said in another way, all problems involve separation and all solutions involve joining.

9. We always have the choice to make any decision regarding what we think to be true or not true, of what we will do or not do, of what we will think or not think. We therefore choose our attitudes; they do not choose us.

10. Life is a process, a classroom, a school in which we learn and grow. Every experience is a learning opportunity. The purpose of life is to learn to practice forgiveness and to share this learning process with others.

As these assumptions became an integral part of my being, so did the meaning of the attitudinal healing principles. These principles are the course of study for healing the mind, experiencing inner peace and seeing the world differently. Understanding, healing and integrating all take place gradually at ever deeper levels. Like the rosebud, there is an unfolding of layers of petals until the full blossom is displayed.

THE TWELVE PRINCIPLES OF ATTITUDINAL HEALING

1. The essence of our being is love.

2. Health is inner peace. Healing is letting go of fear.

3. Giving and receiving are the same.

4. We can let go of the past and of the future.

5. Now is the only time there is and each instant is for giving.

6. We can learn to love ourselves and others by forgiving rather than judging.

7. We can become love-finders rather than fault-finders.

8. We can choose and direct ourselves to be peaceful inside regardless of what is happening outside.

9. We are students and teachers to each other.

10. We can focus on the whole of life rather than the fragments.

11. Since love is eternal, death need not be viewed as fearful.

12. We can always perceive ourselves and others as either extending love or giving a call for help.

Chapter Two

THE TWO TENETS

The night before I began writing the first chapter of this book, I had a dream. In this dream I saw the cover of a book on which was written, "To See Differently – Dostoyevsky." The words, "to see differently," were imbued with a beautiful sound and I kept repeating them over and over, as though they were very sacred. I was extremely comforted by these words. I awoke briefly, continuing to repeat the words and experiencing their healing resonance.

I soon went back to sleep and immediately had a second dream:

> I am with a man from a foreign country (I sense he is Russian) who is on a dangerous mission which involves helping some people in serious difficulty. Time is of the essence. Sitting next to him, I gently and lovingly place my hand on his back. My sole role is to support and comfort him. I do not know any of the details of the mission and feel no need to ask. I feel unconditional love for the man and genuinely trust myself to play my role. I am in a state of equanimity. I know the man will return to his home country once the mission is completed. I feel grateful to be with him even if it is only for a short time.

I had read Dostoyevsky's books *The Idiot* and *The Brothers Karamazov* thirty years ago when I was in graduate school. I have not consciously thought much about Dostoyevsky since then. The morning after these dreams, I immediately went to a bookstore and purchased all the books by him that were available. A brief biographical statement at the beginning of *The Brothers Karamazov* caught my attention:

His life was as dark and dramatic as the great novels he wrote. He was born in Moscow in 1821, the son of a former army surgeon whose drunken brutality led his own serfs to murder him by pouring vodka down his throat until he strangled. A short first novel, *Poor Folk* (1846), brought him instant success, but his writing career was cut short by his arrest for alleged subversion against Tsar Nicholas I in 1849. In prison he was given the "silent treatment" for eight months (guards even wore velvet-soled boots) before he was led in front of a firing squad. Dressed in a death shroud, he faced an open grave and awaited his execution when, suddenly, an order arrived commuting his sentence. He then spent four years at hard labor in a Siberian prison, where he began to suffer from epilepsy, and he only returned to St. Petersburg a full ten years after he had left in chains.

His prison experiences coupled with his conversion to a conservative and profoundly religious philosophy formed the basis for his great novels. But it was his fortuitous marriage to Anna Snikina, following a period of utter destitution brought about by his compulsive gambling, that gave Dostoevsky the emotional stability to complete *Crime and Punishment* (1866), *The Idiot* (1868-69), *The Possessed* (1871-72), and *The Brothers Karamazov* (1879-80). When Dostoevsky died in 1881, he left a legacy of masterworks that influenced the great thinkers and writers of the Western world and immortalized him as a giant among writers of world literature.[1]

Without a doubt, Dostoyevsky had "to see differently" to write his profoundly spiritual and philosophical novels. Rather than indulging in self-pity and withdrawing from life, Dostoyevsky had chosen to explore his life circumstances and to see them as carriers of relevant messages for spiritual growth. He wrote as a way to heal what had happened to him and to do so, he had to investigate how he might see the events and people in life differently.

In searching for the meaning of the first dream, I realized that Dostoyevsky is a profound example of a person who had not only chosen to see differently but had also chosen to share his healing process with others. This is attitudinal healing as practiced a hundred years ago by a literary genius. His healing process is similar to ours; the content of the life stories may differ but the process of healing is the same. The dream indicated not only the title of this book but that it was to reflect both the "seeing" and "sharing" aspects of attitudinal healing.

The second dream, I entitled "Selfless Service." The complete equanimity in the service of another which I experienced in this dream has been a lifetime goal. I realized, however, that there were certain personal attitudes I needed to heal in order to achieve such a goal. I could not possibly experience selfless service if I still carried grievances in my heart, had expectations of others to change or was resistant to participating fully in the process of life. I could not be engaged in selfless service unless I cultivated a profound connection to the Divine Source. This connection was the source of equanimity. I saw, too, that I had to be willing to recognize and perform the duties I had been given to do in this life.

While in India in 1987, I had a dream which I now realize was a prerequisite to "Selfless Service." I had gone to spend the Christmas holidays at an ashram. My increasing responsibilities at the Institute had led me to question my physical, emotional and spiritual strength. I felt I needed to strengthen my spiritual awareness.

My spiritual teacher seemed to know that I was physically and emotionally exhausted. I was placed in a lovely cottage and spent most of my two weeks in solitude and silence. It was during this time that I had the dream that totally reoriented my way of living my life and being of service.

> God, appearing as a stocky middle-aged man, is handing out report cards to a large group of people. I watch Him go from person to person and soon He comes to me. Appearing quite impersonal, He holds up a long piece of paper, and with His finger, He scans down a long list of qualities and traits. He stops in the middle of the list and says, "Susan, you are low in willingness. To run a successful Center you must be totally willing." At first I react with much indignation and say, "How can You say that! I work day and night, I've practically given up my life for what I do." On and on I rave. He waits patiently.

Finally, I stop, become silent and reflect a moment. The truth is I have not totally committed myself to the task of running the Center. Actually, I have not even made a commitment to living my life fully on planet Earth. I am always waiting, not wanting to live one hundred percent for fear there won't be energy left for the "something better" in the future. My attitude is to save my energy for "what my purpose really is," even if the discovery of that is years away. I am not one hundred percent committed to living my life fully one hundred percent of the time. I am holding back the energy of life itself!

So, I say to God, "You're right." And, without a word, He moves on to the next person.

The next morning as my New Year's resolution I prayed that 1988 would bring me an inner state of total willingness to live my life fully and do the task that I was being asked to do. For now, that was running the Center.

One year later, during the Christmas holidays of 1988, I realized the "Selfless Service" dream was also about willingness. This time I experienced my own willingness to serve others. In this dream, I am willing to do the task that needs to be done with unconditional love and with no expectations of results or rewards. A person is in need of support while he is carrying out his mission. My role is solely to provide this support in a loving manner. I have no need to know what the mission is about or even to appraise its value. I am totally willing to play this role as long as the man needs support. When his mission is completed, he will be on his way and so will I. How wonderful it would be to be in that state of mind all the time!

These two sets of dreams and the intervening year demonstrate the two basic tenets of attitudinal healing:

1. the participation in one's own healing process by choosing to see differently and

2. the willingness to extend or share unconditionally that healing with others.

We participate in our own healing process by first choosing to see our life circumstances differently and then doing the inner work necessary to bring the healing about. Dostoyevsky used writing as his method of doing inner work. I choose to do dreamwork, to meditate, to journal and to practice the attitudinal healing principles. The purpose of inner work is to bring harmony and healing to the human psyche. The methods a person selects will differ, depending on his style of learning and the nature of his needs.

Attitudinal healing is also about being of service to others as an extension of our own healing. Dostoyevsky generously shared his healing with others through his novels. There is no doubt that our Institute and all who participate in its activities have benefited from my healed attitude of total willingness. As my willingness grew, so did the breadth and depth of the Institute's programs.

The method of explaining and demonstrating these two tenets to the reader is in keeping with the philosophy of attitudinal healing, namely that we teach through sharing our own healing process. We are the embodiment of what we have learned from our own experience. As we extend that learning to others, we teach who we are. Who we are reflects our life experiences and how we choose to view them.

Chapter Three

THE HEALING PROCESS

Ancient Stoics and modern existentialists like Viktor Frankl recognize that "the last of the human freedoms (is) – to choose one's attitude in a given set of circumstances, to choose one's own way." Frankl goes on to say that "It is this spiritual freedom – that cannot be taken away – that makes life meaningful and purposeful."[1]

Frankl, like Dostoyevsky, experienced severe physical and psychological trauma while imprisoned. His lessons of spiritual freedom were learned in a German concentration camp. The gift which both men have passed on through their writings, is that "man can preserve a vestige of spiritual freedom, of independence of mind, even in such terrible conditions of psychic and physical stress." The lives of these two men exemplify what Frankl calls "attitudinal heroism"[2] – that decision to claim one's right to choose one's attitude when all other choices have been denied.

By not being conscious of this freedom of choice we set limitations on ourselves and others. In setting limitations, we are participating in labeling the world as right-wrong and good-bad and then prioritizing things accordingly. In actuality, there is no order of difficulty in either problems or solutions. This was taught with clarity in a counseling class a friend of mine took.

The professor gave the class a list of "problems" and asked the class to prioritize them. On the list were things like: having Alzheimer's disease, being paralyzed by an accident, death of a child, breakup of a thirty-year marriage, loss of home and possessions to fire, birth of a severely handicapped child and so on. Of course, it took only a few moments to realize that the list could not be organized in order of difficulty.

How "bad" the problem is depends on how it is viewed by the person(s) involved. How a person appears to be handling a problem may differ from his inner reality. Persons who perform heroic acts or survive great sufferings do not see themselves as heroes or as great. They simply did what they felt they had to do in the circumstances. We can never know our own strength until it is tested. People who have been put to the test may become well-known, but they are not different from the rest of us. Just as Neil Armstrong did not, without preparation, awaken one day as an astronaut, Agnes Gonxha Bojaxhiu did not awaken one day as Mother Teresa. Each had to overcome many obstacles and tests along the way.

It may be that it is less difficult to choose "attitudinal heroism" when other choices are denied than it is to choose attitudinal healing when choices seem to abound. A choice for healing is usually precipitated by a crisis that pushes us to the point of "attitudinal heroism" – we feel we have no choice but to change our lives or we will experience psychological or physical death. We all have this final spiritual freedom.

Manuel first came to see me to please his daughter, not out of any conscious interest in healing his attitudes. A cellular biologist at a university, Manuel had spent his entire career in laboratory research. In his early sixties he felt he finally had made a discovery about cellular function that would prove the value of his lifetime of concentrated effort. He had hoped this discovery would lead to a Nobel Prize. He submitted his findings to numerous professional journals in his field, only to have his work repeatedly challenged and rejected. Within six months after his findings had been rejected by his colleagues, Manuel developed melanoma.

Because Manuel lived out of state, we decided that he would come to see me for two intensive days of work. After a gracious greeting, Manuel's first words were, "I don't believe any of this psychological and spiritual stuff. I've come to see you only because I love my daughter. Be prepared for me to challenge every single word you say." Manuel and I sat at my dining room table and began our two-day dialogue. He asked about scientific evidence for a mind-body connection and about what I had found in my own work. I shared what was in the professional literature and what I had observed in my own work with cancer patients. He generously critiqued and dismissed every single idea I shared.

At the end of the two days Manuel surprised me by beginning to question his attitudes. He began examining the quality of his family relationships and the condition of his emotional and spiritual well-being. His family was startled by his intention to return for further appointments. During these subsequent sessions, he gradually confronted the estrangement between himself and his family and shed the guilt he had for the neglect of others and himself. At home he began to share his feelings with his family and to make amends with his wife and children. He began to live his life from his heart rather than from his intellect and he honored himself physically, emotionally and spiritually as well as mentally.

Manuel became happier and more at peace with himself than at any other time in his life. His family relationships transformed. "You know," he said once when we met, "I have this thought and I know you won't think I'm crazy for saying it. You know what I say every day when I wake up now? I say, 'Thank you, melanoma, thank you! You have brought me the gift of happiness and peace with my family.'" Manuel lived several years beyond the predicted time and magnanimously shared his healed attitudes with others. Every Christmas he would call me to share his joy and his continuing process.

Manuel's healing process was a demonstration of "attitudinal heroism." His story demonstrates that the healing of attitudes is a multifaceted process requiring commitment, willingness, persistence, consistency, responsibility, trust and patience. The major stages in the process of healing attitudes are:

Stage One: Questioning Attitudes

Stage Two: Exploring Choices

Stage Three: Making the Commitment

Stage Four: Allowing the Process to Unfold

Stage Five: Acknowledging Healing and Growth

STAGE ONE: QUESTIONING ATTITUDES

Had Manuel not begun to question his long-held attitudes, his last years would have been different. He initially resisted exploring his attitudes and the quality of his life. The first observable "gift" of his cancer was the questioning of his belief system, his attitudes. For sixty years he had identified solely with his intellect and saw his salvation in science. He neglected the other three parts of his being, his physical, emotional and spiritual selves. With the rejection of his life-long scientific "contribution," his life had lost all meaning.

The questioning stage of the healing process often (but not always) begins after an event that shatters the psyche, that loosens thoughts that have become solidified, rigid and inflexible. Movement of energy within the psyche during this questioning stage makes possible a restructuring of the psyche in a more creative and healthy way. This disturbance in the psyche is often referred to as an existential crisis – by definition, a time when a person questions the very meaning and purpose of his life.

Leo Tolstoy has written an illuminating account of his own existential crisis which is a very clear example of the questioning stage of the healing process:

> Five years ago something very strange began to happen to me. At first I experienced moments of perplexity and arrest of life as though I did not know what to do or how to live, and I felt lost and became dejected. But this passed, and I went on living as before. Then these moments of perplexity began to recur more and more often. . .They were always expressed by the questions: What is it for? What does it lead to?

> At first it seemed to me that these were aimless and irrelevant questions. I thought that it was all well-known, and that if I should ever wish to deal with the solution it would not cost me much effort: just at present, I had no time for it, but when I wanted to I should be able to find the answer. The questions however began to repeat themselves frequently and to demand replies more and more insistently. . . I understood that it was something very important; and that if these questions constantly repeated themselves they would have to be answered. And I tried to answer them. The questions seemed such stupid, simple, childish ones; but as soon as I touched them and tried to solve them I at once became convinced, first, that they are not childish and stupid but the most important and profound of life's questions; and secondly that, try as I would, I could not solve them. . .

...when considering plans for the education of my children, I would say to myself: What for?

Or when thinking of the fame my works would bring me, I would say to myself, "Very well, you will be more famous than Gogol or Pushkin or Shakespeare or Moliere, or than all the writers in the world – and what of it?"

And I could find no reply at all. The questions would not wait, they had to be answered at once, and if I did not answer them it was impossible to live. But there was no answer. . .

All around me I had what is considered complete good fortune. I was not yet fifty; I had a good wife who loved me and whom I loved, good children, and a large estate which without much effort on my part improved and increased. I was respected by my relations and acquaintances more than at any previous time. I was praised by others and without much self-deception could consider that my name was famous. And far from being insane or mentally diseased, I enjoyed on the contrary a strength of mind and body such as I have seldom met with among men of my kind; physically I could keep up with the peasants at mowing, and mentally I could work for eight and ten hours at a stretch without experiencing any ill results from such exertion. . .

I felt that what I had been standing on had collapsed, and that I had nothing left under my feet. What I had lived on no longer existed, and there was nothing left.

My life came to a standstill. I could breathe, eat, drink, and sleep, and I could not help doing these things; but there was no life, for there were no wishes the fulfillment of which I could consider reasonable. If I desired anything, I knew in advance that whether I satisfied my desire or not, nothing would come of it. Had a fairy come and offered to fulfill my desires I should not have known what to ask. If in moments of intoxication I felt something which, though not a wish, was a habit left by former wishes, in sober moments I knew this to be a delusion and that there was really nothing to wish for.[3]

The resolution of such a crisis begins when the individual expands the meaning of his existence beyond what is defined by his personality and welcomes the increasing flow of energy from his Higher Self. In other words, a person begins to dis-identify from his personality and ego self and from the environment and expands his identification to include the transpersonal dimension. He develops a growing curiosity about spiritual philosophies, metaphysics or perhaps the implications of modern physics. He basically says there must be another way to look at the world and begins to see that this other way is a spiritual matter.

STAGE TWO: EXPLORING CHOICES

The questioning stage is followed by a period in which one explores his readiness and willingness to make a commitment to participate fully in the healing or restructuring process. It is one thing to question one's view of the self and the world. It is quite another to truly make a commitment to actively explore the unknown, not knowing what the exploration will be like or how it will change one's life.

People often experience great fear at this time. Primarily, there is a fear of loss of everything one has held dear. Commonly, people fear that if they take the step toward healing, that everything in their external lives might change, that they will have to give up their job, their family, their security and so on. Of course, this is not true. As the internal life changes, one may feel a need to change an external circumstance. By then, however, one will view it as a gain, not a "giving up."

Once Manuel recognized that he'd "only been one-fourth alive all these years" it was quite another matter to jump in and address the life-long neglect of his emotional, spiritual and physical needs. At first he felt immobilized with fear and resistance. It was as though he was faced with jumping into a very cold pool of water, knowing that even though doing so would be refreshing, it would initially be frightening and uncomfortable. Manuel, however, began to sense that whatever pain he needed to experience as he healed, it was nothing compared to living the rest of his life without peace.

This stage challenges our willingness to suspend what we think is true in order to explore another way to look at our lives, not knowing where that exploration might lead us. We each must ask, "Am I willing to look in the bag in front of the bag behind me? Can I confront the many unknown and denied parts of myself and begin to dialogue with them? Can I open to the possibility that what I thought was so, may not be? Do I have the patience to 'hang in there' with myself no matter how long or how intense the healing process might be?"

People stay in this exploratory and deliberating stage for varying periods of time, depending on their interest and readiness to move forward. A person with a history of physical and/or psychological abuse especially needs to stay in this stage until he feels psychologically safe to move forward. Extreme fear and confusion relating to the possibility of not being in conscious control challenges the psychological safety of persons who have been abused. Therefore, they must gently prepare themselves for their healing process by cultivating patience and discovering ways to proceed slowly and carefully. Always our Higher Self is available as the guide who gently and wisely leads us through all the stages.

STAGE THREE: MAKING THE COMMITMENT

Once the full commitment is made to the healing of one's attitudes, one may notice a dramatic shift in the intensity and pace of one's process. With this commitment comes a concentrated force of energy within the psyche that mobilizes the breaking down or releasing of old belief systems and allows the psyche to move more quickly toward wholeness.

Manuel made the commitment to his healing process at the end of the first weekend that we worked together. As is often the case when one makes a commitment, the universe began to support Manuel's decision and synchronistic events occurred. His wife and children opened their hearts immediately and were ready to work with him on the healing of family relationships.

With commitment comes empowerment – the ability to assume full responsibility and leadership in one's own healing process. Manuel showed his sense of empowerment by the way that he willingly and fully participated in his process. It was always clear to everyone that Manuel was the master of his life. Empowerment comes from knowing that one's

Higher Self is totally in charge and knows what is best. Feeling empowered is acknowledging the possession of the inner strength and resources needed to participate fully in the healing process, regardless of what might be involved. Empowerment grows in depth and magnitude as one experiences progress in his healing.

STAGE FOUR: ALLOWING THE PROCESS TO UNFOLD

The healing of attitudes is not always a smooth process. There are usually emotional ups and downs along the way. It is important to honor our own pacing and our own ups and downs and to trust that our Higher Self is directing us in our process. It is also important to understand some of the dynamics of the human psyche in the healing process.

There are no rules for how the healing process unfolds except for those we impose on ourself. Rather than focusing on the "how" of our healing process, we need to open ourself to direction from within concerning what will be facilitating for us at any given time. People differ greatly in what is "right" for them.

The human psyche is made up of energy. One of the natural laws of the psyche is that this energy is moved and arranged by our experiences, including the experiences we have in the womb. Our psyche, therefore, needs reinforcement through experience in order to grow and evolve and to maintain its flexibility and its new ways of moving.

New experience that we bring to our psyches has to be integrated in order for the psyche to be healthy, vital and growing. Too much change at one time can cause the psyche to become fragmented so that it cannot integrate the new experience or maintain the flexibility of movement. Often a person experiences fear and confusion when this happens. This is especially true if too much unconscious energy comes to the conscious level too quickly. The healing of the mind is enduring and dynamic when we allow the process to occur in a way that neither increases fear nor breaks through the ego boundaries to such an extent that one feels fragmented and unable to function in daily life.

There are periods of transition in the healing process in which the old pattern is not yet dissolved and the new one is not yet formed and stable. The mind may rebel and resist the change. As a result one may feel worse instead of better. The length of the "feeling worse" period depends on how stubbornly the old attitudes are rooted in the unconscious and how consistently we reinforce new patterning. This transition period takes time and it needs to be reinforced and strengthened through practice. The insight offered by Edgar Cayce that to not apply what we know dissipates energy and undermines the will illustrates the need to reinforce our learning through practice in order to maintain our sense of empowerment.[4]

There are four major ways in which one can support the dissolving of old patterns within the psyche and the developing of a more flexible and energized psyche. The exercises described in later chapters are designed to include these ways of dissolving old patterns.

1. Shedding swallowed tears

From birth we begin developing strategies for meeting our psychological, as well as our physical, needs. When these needs are not met in a nurturing way we develop strategies for dealing with our grief and pain. This takes the form of denial. When we deny the pain, we deny its expression – we literally swallow our tears. These swallowed tears are stored in the psyche and in the body. Shedding these tears releases trapped energy in the psyche and the body, making this energy available for other purposes.

2. Delivering undelivered communications

Another strategy we learn as children is to withhold verbal communications out of fear of rejection or reprisal. Later in life we experience undelivered communications in relationship to spouses, colleagues, teachers, children and even organizations. These undelivered communications form energy blocks within the psyche and need to be released through expression.

3. Releasing suppressed negative emotions

Emotions of anger, guilt and fear can be denied throughout our lives as a way to survive within our environment and in our family. Externalizing these emotions is necessary to release the trapped energy and to create a space for the possibility of forgiveness. It is important as we release angry feelings that we do so in a way that does not create more guilt. In this way, the anger is truly released and is not perpetuated.

4. Owning all parts of ourselves

Polarities in the form of opposites form the dynamics of the psyche. In order for the energy of these polarities to be in balance, one must claim or acknowledge their existence without judgement and condemnation. This means owning our positive and negative qualities, what we like and what we don't like, what we want and what we don't want. It also means accepting the inner child and the inner adolescent with all their vulnerabilities, insecurities and needs. Only when we own or claim all parts of our psyche, the conscious and unconscious, and are in dialogue with these parts, can we be free to choose what part we want to think or express at any given point in time.

Various methods and tools support the unfolding of the healing process. What facilitates one person's process may not facilitate another. The vast number of approaches available for one to choose from is a reflection of the variation among human psyches. The only way to determine which approach is best for you is to ask your Inner Voice to guide you. Manuel, for example, found the tools of meditation, visualization and inspirational reading particularly effective in facilitating his process. The use of imagery in which he dialogued with his inner guide brought him the clearest sense of direction.

Throughout one's healing process it is extremely important to cultivate what is called the Witness Self. The Witness Self observes what is happening yet does not identify with thoughts, emotions, desires or sensations. As Ferrucci says in *What We May Be*:

> We dis-identify by observing. Instead of being absorbed by sensations, feelings, desires, thoughts, we observe them objectively without judging them, without wanting to change them, without interfering with them in any way. We see them as distinct from us, as if we were looking at a landscape.

> This attitude of serene observation can be practiced at any moment of our life, and its first effect is that of liberation. I am fearful, I observe my fear, I see its contours clearly, I see that the fear is not me, that it is a thing outside myself; I am free of that fear.

...the (observer) self is the part in us that can watch any content of the psyche without getting caught up in its atmosphere. This fact allows the whole personality to find a balance of which it would not otherwise be capable.[5]

Ram Dass and Paul Gorman in their book *How Can I Help?* further describe the Witness Self:

If we imagine that our mind is like the blue sky, and that across it pass thoughts as clouds, we can get a feel for that part of it which is other than our thoughts. The sky is always present; it contains the clouds and yet is not contained by them. So with our awareness. It is present and encompasses all our thoughts, feelings, and sensations; yet it is not the same as them. To recognize and acknowledge this awareness, with its spacious, peaceful quality, is to find a very useful resource within. We see that we need not identify with each thought just because it happens to occur. We can remain quiet and choose which thought we wish to attend to. And we can remain aware *behind* all these thoughts, in a state that offers an entirely new level of openness and insight.[6]

When we observe or witness the ups and downs in our healing process rather than becoming them, we feel reassured and strengthened. Cultivating the awareness of the Witness Self is our anchor during the times in our healing process when we fear getting lost in the pain and suffering. It also allows us to monitor our progress, to recognize our next step in healing and to reinforce new patterns.

STAGE FIVE: ACKNOWLEDGING HEALING AND GROWTH

Acknowledging our growth steps to ourselves is extremely important for the health and well-being of our psyches. By acknowledging our own efforts and our own growth, we are welcoming nurturance and completion into our psyche. Our work is validated and our inner sense of direction is affirmed. Acknowledgement also becomes a teacher for us by showing us the individual steps and patterns of our unique healing process.

Each step, no matter how small we perceive it, should be acknowledged verbally, out loud to ourselves. This can be done while looking in a mirror or repetitively while driving the car. Oral acknowledgement and repetition strengthen our growth.

Another way to strengthen what we have learned and gained is to acknowledge our growth to another trusted person. Manuel's call at Christmas was his way of affirming his own continued healing and of having it strengthened through sharing.

The healing process is not linear in time; it is more a spiral into the depths of the psyche which continues to move and expand with each affirmation of "attitudinal heroism." As we reach one level of understanding, a new awareness will arise. As we recommit to our own growth, we allow the process to unfold over and over again on different issues or on the same issue at ever deeper levels.

Chapter Four

BEING OF SERVICE

THE INTENTION OF SERVICE

In a dream, God told King Solomon that he could have anything he wanted. King Solomon, realizing he did not know how to guide his kingdom, asked for an understanding heart so that he could serve his people by discerning right from wrong. God was so pleased that King Solomon had asked for wisdom that he also gave him what he didn't ask for – riches and honor. God then told King Solomon what he needed to do (and not to do) to retain this wisdom throughout his life.

King Solomon soon became known for quickly and wisely solving thousands of problems brought before him. The best known report of his wisdom involved two prostitutes who each claimed to be the mother of a certain baby boy. Both recently had given birth to sons but during the night one prostitute had suffocated her baby by accidently lying on him. King Solomon, in his wisdom, asked for a sword to divide the surviving baby in half. The real mother quickly begged him not to do so. In this way, he knew which woman was truly the baby's mother and gave him to her.

The Queen of Sheba heard of King Solomon's wisdom and prosperity and came to see for herself if the stories were true. She concluded that his wisdom and prosperity exceeded even his fame that had spread abroad. She saw for herself that "happy are thy men, happy are these thy servants, which span continually before thee, and that hear thy wisdom."[1]

As time passed, King Solomon began to become more devoted to increasing his power and riches and less interested in serving his kingdom with an understanding heart. For years he demanded that thousands of slaves serve him by building his golden temple and palace and tilling his land. He also forgot to honor God's requests for guarding his gift of wisdom. He died with his kingdom destroyed by his change of intention from serving spiritual values to serving physical pleasures and material riches. After his death, the people whom Sheba had once seen as happy, asked his son Rehoboam to "make the yoke which thy father did put upon us lighter."[2]

The story of King Solomon's life is an example of the two levels on which we serve others. First, we are all unconsciously and unintentionally in a constant state of service through the example of our lives. As we become more conscious of this level of service and as we develop our own inner peace, we move into the second level of service in which service becomes an act of intention from the heart. At this level, service manifests as love in action. We can slip back into serving only unintentionally if, like Solomon, we are not vigilant about our intention.

Our Constant State of Service

Because it is the human condition to be in relationship with others, we are in a constant state of service. My friend and colleague, Peggy Tabor Millin, recalls a visual metaphor which graphically reminds us that we serve even when we are not conscious of serving.

> I was on a train on a rainy day. The train was slowing down to pull into a station. For some reason I became intent on watching the raindrops on the window. Two separate drops, pushed by the wind, merged into one for a moment and then divided again – each carrying with it a part of the other. Simply by that momentary touching, neither was what it had been before. And as each one went on to touch other raindrops, it shared not only itself, but what it had gleaned from the other. I saw this metaphor many years ago and it is one of my most vivid memories. I realized then that we never touch people so lightly that we do not leave a trace. Our state of being matters to those around us, so we need to become conscious of what we unintentionally share so we can learn to share with intention.

As long as King Solomon served with intentionality through alignment with God's purpose, his people were happy. His mere presence as leader was enough to ensure happiness as long as he was acting from his heart. Once he began to feel and to act as if he, Solomon, were the true source of his wisdom and prosperity, he fell from grace and his people felt his rule like a yoke around their necks.

Practicing attitudinal healing raises our consciousness of how we are unintentionally always of service to others. People glean insights and understandings by observing how we think, react and live. We serve others simply by existing. We don't have to intentionally do, say or be anything. When we are at peace within ourselves, we share peace simply by being.

Much of our learning and way of being in this world is a reflection of the peer and adult models we have had in our lives. Solomon had learned from his father, David, "to walk in the way of the Lord."[3] This provided him a model so that when God spoke to him in a dream, he listened, and when God gave him a choice, Solomon made a wise one. When he grew older, he forgot his father's way and, tantalized by models of fame and wealth, took a different path.

Joseph Chilton Pearce, a world-renowned child development specialist, and Alice Miller, a psychoanalyst specializing in adults with abusive childhoods, stress the extraordinary impact that adults have on the perceptions of children.[4] Both agree that who we are as adults is a direct reflection of the modeling we experienced throughout infancy and childhood. They feel it is vital to have healthy peer and adult models throughout our lives to guide us in our physical, mental, emotional and spiritual development. Without the opportunity to learn from effective models – people who are developmentally one step ahead of us – an individual may become confused, anxious and lacking in understanding and purpose.

We experience others as models and are models ourselves every day of our lives. Like the raindrops, we touch and are touched by one another. The touching may occur through the media or in a book or simply in overhearing a remark. People in all walks of life – street vendors, a homeless person in the subway, the news broadcaster, a postal clerk – all serve us and are served by us in return. By our own lives we are in constant service, modeling for others our state of consciousness and being.

Serving With Intentionality

Being of service within the philosophical framework of attitudinal healing also includes very specific and direct ways of being, saying and doing. In attitudinal healing, we serve others as a natural extension of our own healing and from the intention to serve. We serve from a place of unconditional love and honor for the other person's process. We join with and support others without expectations of results and without having to consciously know their needs. We facilitate a person from a place of inner direction; therefore, what we say or do or do not say or do will vary from person to person.

The intentional level of being of service within the context of attitudinal healing includes both our state of being and our love in action.

The life of Brother Lawrence is an excellent example of the intentional level of serving through one's state of being. Brother Lawrence, a Carmelite lay-brother, lived in an obscure monastery in Europe in the 1600's. He spent his youth as a soldier and, when captured by the enemy, was falsely accused as a spy. He was not hanged because his total indifference to death convinced his captors of his innocence. Upon rejoining his own forces, he was wounded and during convalescence decided to abandon his arms and join a monastery. For many years he suffered great anguish as he searched for peace of mind. After having an experience in which he "perceived a ray of divine light which, illuminating his spirit, dissipated all his fears, and ended his pain,"[5] Brother Lawrence lived out his life in that light.

Whatever Brother Lawrence did – make omelets, pick a straw from the floor or repair shoes – he emanated the presence of this light. People came great distances just to be in his presence. As in attitudinal healing, Brother Lawrence's way of being of service was not what he did, but his state of mind when he did it. His way of being was one form of love in action that served others.

Peace Pilgrim is an example of someone who intentionally served others through her state of being and her choice of action. Until her death in 1981, Peace Pilgrim walked back and forth across America with the goal of walking for peace until there was peace in the world. Wherever she walked, she met people who were attracted to her peacefulness. On several occasions, people admitted that they had approached her meaning harm but her sense of peace had changed their minds. Her physical needs were always met without her asking. As she gave of her peace, people responded with food and shelter. She was asked to come off the road to give talks on the radio and in school auditoriums. She taught what she had learned – that peace begins within the individual and only then can extend outward to the world. She also demonstrated for us one form of service that love in action can take.[6]

Love, as defined by Scott Peck, is "the will to extend one's self for the purpose of nurturing one's own or another's spiritual growth."[7] To love is to be willing to extend one's hand to another, to be present in a way that empowers the person to draw upon his own inner strengths and potentialities, to be his own best therapist. Ferrucci says,

> *Service is love in action,* deliberately and creatively applied and circulated. We love or serve other people by eliciting their resources, by understanding, by transmitting vision, by healing an emotional wound, by education, and in innumerable other ways, at all levels – from the physical to the spiritual.[8]

Many of us feel a calling to serve others. Some of us are called upon to support family and friends. Others choose to serve in helping professions or feel guided to seek opportunities to extend support to others within the community. Regardless of our life circumstance, we can choose to view our lives as an opportunity to give to others in a way that reflects our own unique self and in a way that expresses love in action.

ATTRIBUTES OF SERVICE

There are nine attributes which characterize the levels of being of service within the philosophy of attitudinal healing.

1. Constancy

We serve others by virtue of our existence alone and without seemingly intending to do so. Regardless of our life circumstance or what we do or say, we offer to others the opportunity to learn from the example of our lives. In this way, we are constantly being of service to others.

2. Deliberateness

We can consciously intend to serve others, deliberately extending our hand to another for the purpose of nurturing another's physical, mental, emotional or spiritual growth.

3. Love

Love is the atmosphere or energy field within which being of service takes place. The belief that love is the essence of all human beings lies behind our motives for serving others.

4. Wisdom

When our intention to serve is clear, we operate from our hearts with love and follow the guidance we receive with meticulous integrity. We serve with wisdom and understanding.

5. Extension

We serve others by extending our state of mind. If the energy which emanates from our presence is uplifting, we will uplift others. If our energy is clear and peaceful, those around us will experience a greater sense of clarity and peace.

6. Reciprocity

There is a reciprocal relationship between personal healing and serving others. As we heal, we naturally extend the energy of that healing to others. This extension strengthens our own healing.

7. Empowerment

Being of service is to empower the person to draw upon his own inner strengths and potentialities, to be his own best therapist. We do not have to worry about what to say or do as long as we ask within for guidance about any given situation; in this way, we are not the doer and we are assured the highest good is served for all. When the highest good is served, the person will feel empowered.

8. Multiplicity

There are many forms of service, on physical, mental, emotional and spiritual levels. One can mow the lawn of a neighbor who is ill, tutor inmates in prison, listen on the hotline, pray for someone, be a musician or artist, do needlework, arrange flowers, cook meals, be a friend, be a grocery clerk, be a psychotherapist.

9. Individuality

The manner that being of service takes is a reflection of the person's

motivation, intentionality, unique gifts, personality and life purpose. The style of serving is unique for each person because we as
human beings are unique.

FACILITATION: SERVICE THROUGH ACTIVE SUPPORT OF OTHERS

Facilitate and *facilitator* are terms used throughout this book to
describe the unique dynamic of the supportive process within the context
of attitudinal healing. To facilitate simply means "to make easy." The
role of the facilitator is to create a supportive atmosphere in which a
person can find his own answers with greater ease than he could on his
own. A facilitator in attitudinal healing is aware of the attributes of
service and of viewing service both as a state of mind and as love in action.
Anyone can learn to facilitate someone else. Attitudinal healing facilitators are not counselors or therapists. They are ordinary people.
To assist facilitators in clarifying their intentions in the active
practice of the attitudinal healing principles, eight guidelines have been
developed.

1. Our purpose is to give mutual support through nonjudgemental listening and sharing.

2. By taking the risk of exposing our emotional states, we find
   common experiences that facilitate joining.

3. We look at each other, seeing only the "light" and not the
   "lampshade."

4. We support others as they find their own answers; we do not
   give advice or counseling.

5. We each rely on our own Inner Voice for guidance and answers.

6. It is okay not to have the answers for someone else. The
   intention to extend love is enough.

7. We are here for our own healing; as we are healed we extend
   that healing to others.

8. In each situation, we choose peace by practicing forgiveness and letting go of fear.[9]

The facilitator guidelines are relevant to most situations in which one wishes to be supportive. The only instances in which the guidelines are not appropriate are those which necessitate direct lifesaving intervention, such as threats of suicide or bodily harm and the active practice of substance abuse. Once a person is in the recovery phase of the crisis, supporting a person within the framework of the guidelines can be extremely helpful and effective.

THE QUALITY OF SERVICE

There are three major factors that will affect the quality and effectiveness of your support of another person: creating a safe space, honoring the process and staying on purpose.

Creating a Safe Space

Guideline 1:   Our purpose is to give mutual support through nonjudgemental listening and sharing.

Guideline 2:   By taking the risk of exposing our emotional states, we find common experiences that facilitate joining.

Guideline 3:   We look at each other, seeing only the "light" and not the "lampshade"

Not too long ago, I received a rather frantic phone call from a woman who was very concerned about a friend who had been recently diagnosed as having breast cancer. She said she needed help in knowing "what to do" because her friend was not following through on her suggestions. Her question to me was, "How can I get my friend to listen to me? There are so many things she can do to get well and she won't do them. How can her friends help her when she won't let herself be helped?"

In the course of the conversation, I learned that the woman had seen herself as helpful and supportive by showering her friend with tapes, books and a myriad of holistic health alternatives. I also sensed her own personal fears, anxieties and guilt about her friend's illness. She desperately wanted to have her friend "fixed." When I asked her what her friend's feelings were about the diagnosis, she said, "Oh, she won't talk about them and she won't do anything!"

The foundation of the supportive process is the creation of a safe space for oneself and the person one wishes to support. From this space one can respond with wisdom and clarity to that person's "call for help." The person has to feel emotionally safe before he will share honest thoughts and feelings.

A person will feel emotionally safe when he:

1. Does not feel judged, categorized, compared, evaluated or corrected.

2. Feels totally listened to as though no one else exists in the world and feels that his listener believes that nothing is more important than this moment of interaction.

3. Feels complete with what he has to say or emote.

4. Knows what is said is kept in confidence.

5. Feels his own experience is important and unique because the listener conveys understanding through active listening.

6. Feels a connection, a joining with the listener in some way so there is not a sense of me-you, strong-weak, inferior-superior separation.

To be successful in creating a safe emotional environment for another person, one:

1. Is willing to set aside one's own emotional needs in order to be fully present with the person. Being fully present is communicated by having good eye contact, not interjecting personal stories and experiences, not giving advice and not interpreting what the person is saying.

2. Actively participates in one's own emotional healing process so that a) he does not react in a way that becomes part of the

problem rather than part of the solution and b) what he communicates comes from integrity and honesty and not from denial or deception regarding the condition of his own mind.

3. Acknowledges the presented situation yet sees beyond it, seeing the person as whole, healed, a divine being, a brother or sister.

4. Joins in a common purpose with the person in some way. This can consist of simply being a listener or providing active support such as doing an errand, giving a massage or cooking a dinner.

5. Trusts oneself, knowing one is genuinely willing and desiring to be with the person.

6. Is intuitive and connects with an awareness of one's inner wisdom for guidance.

7. Shares one's own life experiences only to facilitate the supportive process and not to exemplify advice.

When a person says to me, "You are so safe to be with," I realize that I am safe to be with because it feels safe to be with myself. When a person has a sense of being comfortable with himself, then others will feel safe in his presence. A quick assessment of how safe one feels with himself can be done by examining how he spends time alone. Being able to spend time alone in a way that is meaningful, constructive, contemplative and peaceful reflects a feeling of safety with oneself.

In addition, our safety of self includes how safe we feel with certain issues like anger, death, betrayal and so on. Unless we feel safe with the issue ourselves, we cannot provide a safe space for someone else to work on that issue. The safety of self is naturally communicated with others nonverbally and through the joining of minds, so it is important for a facilitator to be honest about his level of safety with various issues.

Honoring the Process

Guideline 4:   We support others as they find their own answers; we do not give advice or counseling.

Guideline 5:   We each rely on our own Inner Voice for guidance and answers.

To trust and honor other people's healing and growing process is to empower them. It is to believe in them and to open our heart to them. It is to recognize their basic goodness and strength. It is seeing beyond the personality. When we see others as having all the inner resources that they need to learn, grow and heal, we create the space for them to be in communication with the wise part of themselves and to discover their unique selves.

True learning emerges out of our life circumstances and how we respond and react to them. To learn, we must have our own inner and outer experiences and make our own choices. We are free to choose our attitude in any circumstance even if we think our choice is a "mistake." As a colleague of mine once said, "Mistakes are not mistakes but steps toward learning." Honoring the process is another means to honor the "mistakes" we have made as steps in the learning process. Making our own choices and being accountable for them strengthens us emotionally and spiritually, deepening our connection to our own inner wisdom.

Listening to our wise Inner Voice for guidance and direction leads to a life of courage, strength and equanimity. Each person has an Inner Voice that carries and expresses the wisdom needed in any given life circumstance. We become our own best therapists as we learn to listen to and follow this Inner Voice. This is how we care for our psychological and spiritual well-being.

We may be tempted to give advice or offer interpretations and recommendations to a person seeking support. A part of us wishes the difficulty were solved quickly so the person could feel better and we could feel better too. We need to be watchful not to impose our will upon the person. Honoring a person's process means honoring his freedom to make his own choices and to be responsible for them. Ann Landers recently wrote in her well-known advice column, "After 33 years I still find writing this column immensely rewarding. I realize that many people who write to me don't want advice. They just need someone who will listen to them."[10]

One of the most beautiful affirmations of honoring another person's process is expressed in the following poem by Theodore Roszak:

> You and I, we meet as strangers,
> Each carrying a mystery within us.
> I may never know who you are,
> I may never know you completely.
> But I trust that you are a person in your own right
> possessed of a beauty and value that are earth's
> richest treasures.

So, I make this promise to you.
I will impose no identities upon you but will invite
you to become yourself without shame or fear.
I will hold open a space for you in the world and
defend your right to fill it with an authentic vocation.
For as long as your search takes,
You have my loyalty.[11]

I have had the good fortune of being supported in the spirit of this vow and have experienced the extent and depth of my own healing from such relationships. The spirit of this vow honors one's own process as well as that of another.

One must practice becoming consciously aware of his process and honoring his own "truth" regardless of the lack of agreement in the outside world. This was made clear to me through an incident with my twenty-year-old Volvo. I had just had its engine rebuilt when I decided to drive it to my parents' home in Indiana. Five hundred miles from Washington, D. C., the car's electrical system suddenly stopped working. When I stopped the car and asked within if the situation was a serious one, I saw in my mind two wires hitting one another. When I asked myself what was wrong with the car, I heard the words, "not much." Questioning this message, I began the odyssey of taking the car to several gas stations and repair shops. I was consistently told that the car's electrical system needed major repair but because of the age of the car, no parts were available. The costs quoted were astronomical – it didn't sound like "not much" to me. A Volvo station in Chicago finally diagnosed the problem – the windshield wiper motor had burned out. After an unsuccessful search for a motor replacement in numerous junk yards, I had to drive back to Washington with a faulty electrical system.

Throughout this episode, I became increasingly confused and discouraged about the validity of my Inner Voice. I gave my power away, so to speak, as I yielded to believing others rather than myself. From this one incident, I found myself questioning my inner guidance process totally.

Upon returning to Washington, I took my car to its usual mechanic. Later in the day the mechanic called and when I asked him what was wrong, he said, "Well, *not much!* A wire from the speedometer and a wire from the windshield wiper system were touching. I taped them – it will cost five dollars to repair it."

The learning involved in this event was not about the variations of opinions in the world of mechanics. My lesson involved trusting and

honoring my process instead of negating it because someone had a
different viewpoint.

To be successful in honoring the process for another person, one:

1. Encourages him to cultivate listening within for his own guidance and solutions to issues. (Guidelines for this are in Chapter
Sixteen.)

2. Refrains from giving suggestions and offering advice.

3. Does not assume that one's own experiences and one's perceptions of them are identical to his.

4. Does not evaluate or judge the choices he makes as being right
or wrong but simply sees them as being choices in the learning
process.

5. Respects the pacing or timing of his process as being right for
him.

6. Trusts that his Higher Self is fully in charge of his process.

7. Does not take responsibility for his choices and decisions.

Staying on Purpose

Guideline 6:   It is okay not to have the answers for someone
else. The intention to extend love is enough.

Guideline 7:   We are here for our own healing; as we are
healed we extend that healing to others.

Guideline 8:   In each situation, we choose peace by practicing
forgiveness and letting go of fear.

These three guidelines state the purpose of facilitation, a purpose
that assures the integrity of the relationship. Each partner in the relationship is both student and teacher for the other, practicing reciprocal giving
and receiving. The purpose of every interaction is to have an opportunity

to practice choosing peace through forgiving ourselves and others. The purpose is to extend love, to keep one's heart open to the other person. When the supportive relationship stays on purpose, both parties feel emotionally safe and the healing process is honored.

I was in the midst of writing a manual for training facilitators, when Phil called wanting to see me for a counseling session. At the time that he called I had been experiencing intense anxiety about a writer's block. Thirteen years before I had had a very wounding experience while writing my doctoral dissertation and since that time had felt much resistance and anxiety when writing professional material.

For three months, I had been unable to write a single word. I suffered silently, using every healing method I knew to try to break through my block. The morning of Phil's call I had felt much desperation and had "given up." I pleaded for help during my morning meditation.

I told Phil I could not see him. I had phased out my private practice and reduced my work load in order to devote all my energies to writing the manual. I did not tell him of my writing anxiety. He began to plead with me to see him, saying that he only needed to see me once, that he just knew I was the person to help him. With a sense of resignation, I said, "Well, what do you want to see me about?" "I have writer's block," he said, "I am a university professor and if I don't start writing some academic papers soon my position will be in jeopardy." I agreed to see Phil.

It was through my work with Phil on his writer's block that I worked through mine. I saw that I had completely brought my trauma of thirteen years ago into the present. I was reliving it because I had not healed the memory. After Phil left, I knew what to do. I had to affirm and reaffirm that I was in the present, in 1985, on this day, in this house, with this typewriter. The writing I wanted to do was a reflection of my own devotional life, so I also needed to make my writing space a devotional area. Phil and I were teachers and students for one another. We experienced the gift of giving and receiving. We stayed on purpose in the supportive relationship.

Staying on purpose also means focusing on choosing to keep one's heart open and extending love when supporting others. Blanche and Everard, two of our Institute facilitators, were begged by a teacher to work with her class of disturbed adolescents. This class was made up of children who had been expelled from other schools and who were in and out of the court system. The teacher was at her "wit's end"; no one seemed able to help these youngsters. The class members had physically thrown one psychologist out of the classroom.

The first thing that Blanche and Everard did was to divide the class into several groups of two. In separate rooms, they began teaching the attitudinal healing principles in a very elementary way. Within four weeks, they risked combining the children for their sessions. The teacher noted the class had improved in that four-week period.

In the class was a girl who seemed to be the class leader and "who could have been on a football team, she was so large and strong." One day Blanche was sitting next to her during a visualization exercise when the girl became agitated. Blanche and Everard had been told that when this girl became agitated, she began throwing chairs and desks, breaking objects, screaming and destroying everything in her path. The teacher and class were always forewarned of such an outburst because the girl would start huffing and puffing just before an episode.

When Blanche realized the girl was about to go out of control, she first tried to stop thinking about what the teacher had said would happen. Then, without looking at the girl, Blanche thought of her as a totally loving being and gently reached out and touched the girl. The girl calmed down and did not lose control.

Some weeks later when Blanche and Everard decided to end their time with the class, this particular girl surprised them by saying, "You aren't going to leave us, are you?"

To be successful in staying on purpose with a person, one:

1. Reaffirms one's purpose for supporting someone prior to being with him and throughout the time together.

2. Knows that loving thoughts can impact on people and situations.

3. Reaffirms the facilitator guidelines prior to being with him and follows them throughout the time together.

4. Acknowledges the value of recentering whenever feeling off purpose.

5. Periodically clarifies and evaluates the value and effectiveness of the supportive relationship with the person being supported, bringing the relationship back on purpose if necessary.

Using the eight facilitating guidelines in service to others as well as in personal and work relationships is empowering and nurturing for one's emotional and spiritual well-being. At our Institute the guidelines help us maintain the purpose and focus of all of our activities, whether it be in a support group, administrative meeting, in a telephone conversation, training class, individual facilitation or our relationships with one another. Along with awareness of the levels and attributes of service, practice of the guidelines supports anyone who wishes to grow personally and to serve others.

PART TWO

The Twelve Principles

Chapter Five

I have seen the truth. It is not as though I had invented it with my mind. I have seen it, SEEN IT, and the living image of it has filled my soul forever....In one day, one hour, everything could be arranged at once. THE CHIEF THING IS TO LOVE.

Fyodor Dostoyevsky

Principle One

THE ESSENCE OF OUR BEING IS LOVE

BASIC TENETS

1. *Each individual is a spark from the universal light; this spark is our essence.*

2. *Love is the ultimate and highest goal to which we can aspire.*

3. *Love is a given, a permanent energy in the universe and in each human being; it is our natural state.*

4. *Loving is looking beyond appearances, beyond the personality and beyond any specialness in our relationships.*

5. *Negative emotions and attitudes block the awareness of the presence of love within ourselves and others.*

6. *Love is reflected back to us and triggers the awareness of love within ourselves.*

7. *Meditation and contemplation strengthen the awareness of our essence of love.*

8. *The most prevalent obstacle to the awareness of love's presence is self-doubt.*

9. *The awareness of our love essence is increased as we extend that love to others.*

10. *Love is the healer.*

THE PRINCIPLE'S MESSAGE

The first attitudinal healing principle includes the remaining eleven. It serves as the arms that hold and embrace them all. The principle confronts us by asking that we address and change the core belief of what we feel our true essence to be. This is not an easy task because most of us are deeply convinced that our inherent state is one of worthlessness and inadequacy. As a great saint once said, mankind's greatest addiction is not alcohol or drugs but the emotional addiction of self-doubt.

Essence is defined by Webster as "the permanent as contrasted with the accidental element of being."[1] This principle tells us that love is the permanent element. Love is the gift we have been given; it is our natural state. Each of us has this gift of love to the same degree and from the same Source. What differs is our awareness of the gift. Our awareness of our love essence increases as we release our self-doubt and as we share our love with others. It is this gift of love, present even if we are totally unaware, that unites us with one another and with the Divine Source.

At the time I was preparing the manuscript for this particular principle, I had already finished reading Dostoyevsky's *The Idiot* and was midway through *The Brothers Karamazov*. Just as my dream had foretold, I was clearly seeing the connection of Dostoyevsky's novels to attitudinal healing and I was experiencing his works as a guiding light for my own writing.

The Brothers Karamazov, Dostoyevsky's last and most inspiring work, contains many philosophical and spiritual treatises on various subjects, including one on universal love, spoken by the character Father Zosima on his deathbed. Father Zosima, a revered monk-priest with extraordinary wisdom and healing powers, was a beloved spiritual teacher of the novice, Alexei. Alexei, the youngest brother, is very mystical in nature, as contrasted to his sensualist brother, Dimitry, his intellectual brother, Ivan, and his tormented half-brother, Smerdyakov.

Alexei records Father Zosima's farewell words to his fellow monks:

> Love God's creation, love every atom of it separately,
> and love it also as a whole; love every green leaf,
> every ray of God's light; love the animals and the
> plants and love every inanimate object. If you come
> to love all things, you will perceive God's mystery
> inherent in all things; once you have perceived it,
> you will understand it better and better every day.
> And finally you will love the whole world with a
> total, universal love.[2]

Prior to this, Father Zosima had met with the Karamazov brothers and their father with the hope of bringing resolution to the family's extreme conflict. At the end of this meeting, Father Zosima suddenly bowed to Dimitry, so reverently that his forehead touched the ground. Later he told Alexei that he saw Dimitry as having murder in his heart. By bowing with such high regard, the monk was honoring and acknowledging Dimitry's inner essence of love. He hoped that this gesture would spark Dimitry's awareness of his true essence and that therefore the crime would not come to pass.

All of Dostoyevsky's characters are dramatic examples of the contrast between love and fear. The characters coming from their love essence are Dostoyevksy's heroes, such as Alexei in *The Brothers Karamazov* and Myshkin in *The Idiot*. Most of Dostoyevksy's characters, however, are in a state of fear, as they wrestle with the question of the existence of God, their love essence.

In the context of attitudinal healing, all negative emotions such as self-doubt, jealousy, confusion, anger, resentment and condemnation are viewed as forms of fear. Fear stems from the belief that our minds have separated from our Source and from one another. Because we find this belief unbearable, we deny it by repressing it into the unconscious. We then project this repressed fear in the form of some attack onto others or things. In contrast, love is not projected; it is extended to others. Because it is our natural state of being, it has no opposite emotion.

How does one experience the reality of love's presence if there is conflict, turmoil and struggle in one's mind? Sometimes we have to begin very simply and allow that essence to be mirrored back to us through something or someone. Kenneth Wapnick shares that the music of Beethoven and Mozart served as the first experience of his own love essence.[3] Well-known now is the healing effect animals have on mentally ill and geriatric patients; the animals serve to spark that inner awareness of love for these people.

When working on any of the principles, we must begin from a place of honesty. With this principle, just desiring to see the love essence in another does not make the seeing easy or automatic. Sometimes even the desire to see it, is not present. As someone once said to me, "I want *to want* TO WANT to see the love essence in my mother but right now I don't!" The person was beginning to work with this principle with an honest statement of her level of willingness, a healthy and vital first step towards seeing her mother differently.

We spend so much time telling ourselves and others what we and they are not. It is vitally important to affirm what we and they are in truth. We must consciously look for evidence of the love essence wherever we can – in music, nature, animals or another person. And we must state our present conflictual attitude honestly so that we can create the possibility of moving forward to a more peaceful one.

WHAT IS MY ATTITUDE?

Contemplate the following questions and write about your feelings in a journal.

1. How would I describe the awareness I have about my inner essence as defined by this principle?

2. Who in my life, either living or dead, do or did I perceive reflecting this essence back to me?

3. With what or whom in my life do I seem to forget the awareness of my own essence?

4. What are my attitudes that serve as obstacles or barriers to experiencing my own essence?

5. What are my attitudes that serve as obstacles or barriers to my seeing the essence of others?

6. How willing am I to recognize my own and others' love essence?

7. Do I devote any time during the day to remembering or reflecting upon the awareness of my true essence, such as in meditation or contemplation?

PRACTICING THE PRINCIPLE

Select the exercises that best facilitate and support your healing process, writing your responses in a journal. You may want to prerecord the visualization exercises.

1. The practice of connecting to the love essence within yourself is essential to fully integrating this principle into your life. The most direct, efficient and meaningful way to do this is through meditation. Starting the day with meditation sets the tone for the day. Even if your meditation time seems fretful to you and your thoughts are rampant, meditation will have a positive influence on how you experience yourself and your relationships throughout the day.

Meditation is a silent, inward focusing of attention and serves as a way to deepen the contact with your inner spiritual reality. In meditation, you reach into the depths of your inner life and go beyond any doctrines or beliefs.

There are many forms of meditation and you may already have a method that you use and prefer. Should this not be so, I would like to recommend the use of the mantra, "hamsa," which means "I am That, That I am." This is a natural mantra, in that these are the sounds we make as we breathe, with "ham" on inhalation, "sa" on exhalation. A mantra is a portion of a sacred text that is chanted, spoken or intoned as a prayer.

Instructions for the Hamsa Mantra:

- Sit upright on a straight chair with feet on the floor or in a cross-legged position on the floor or chair. Clasp hands gently in your lap or join the index finger and thumb of each hand and place the hands on your knees. Keep the spine straight but comfortably so.

- Close your eyes. Breathe naturally.

- Repeat the mantra silently, ham (pronounced h-ah-m) on inhalation, sa (pronounced s-ah) on exhalation.

- Concentrate on the mantra and become absorbed in it. When you are distracted by thoughts, feelings or noises, gently bring your attention back to the mantra.

- Meditate now for 20 minutes.

- Slowly bring yourself back into awareness and open your eyes. You may want to sit in silence a few moments and reflect upon your forthcoming day and what you would like to see it as being.

One can start and end the day with meditation. I also find it helpful to periodically throughout the day spend a few moments in silence to reconnect to the awareness of my inner, quiet reality.

2. Visualization and guided imagery are two useful tools in the healing of the mind. Visualization is the technique of seeing with the mind's eye a self-created image or images. Many athletes use visualization to "create" their performances prior to the actual event. Guided imagery is simply a visualization guided from the outside. The purpose of guided imagery is usually to bring to conscious awareness feelings and experiences from the subconscious.

People experience visualizations in different ways. Many people do not *see* the images as much as they *sense* the images; others *see* with the same clarity with which they *see* a dream. Give yourself the permission to experience visualization in whatever way is uniquely yours; do not evaluate your performance as compared with others. One's experience of visualization changes with practice. Initially your mind may wander. It will be helpful to spend a few minutes in meditation to quiet the mind before beginning a visualization.

As it is difficult to both read and visualize at the same time, you may want to prerecord the visualization exercises. Allow plenty of time to process each step. It may take several trials to produce a taped version that is paced well for your processing.

Guided imagery exercise:

Close your eyes and picture yourself standing in front of you. See yourself as you are now, and note the expression on your face and what your body seems to be communicating.

Now see a beautiful blue-white glow emanating from the heart of this you in front of you. As the blue-white glow grows and expands, this you becomes beautiful and joyous, emotionally strong and serene, knowing all is right and good. Acknowledge the beauty of this you and know that it *is* you.

Gently open your eyes and carry this memory of you throughout the day. Think of this person as being you, so that what you say and do throughout the day comes from that awareness. If you forget, gently recall the image and remind yourself of its qualities.

3. Select something that serves to remind you of your essence and place it in your living or work environment or carry it with you. This may be a picture, a small gift you have been given, a card you have found or have been given, a pendant, a small crystal, a burning candle or any other meaningful reminder.

4. On a sheet of paper, list as thoroughly as possible any barrier you have to seeing your love essence. Then list all the barriers you have to seeing the love essence of others. Are these lists the same or different? After you feel complete with the lists, throw them away!

5. Purposely search for evidence of the existence of the love essence of others, particularly in those towards whom you feel a grievance or in whose presence you feel uncomfortable. This may require your looking for a glimpse, a gesture, a verbal or nonverbal expression. Note any resistance you may have to doing this exercise. Focus on being willing to see the essence and then observing it, rather than forcing yourself to see it.

6. Read something every day that you find inspiring and allow the reading to strengthen the awareness of your love essence. Reading uplifting and inspiring material just before sleep assures a more peaceful night's rest and a more joyous morning the next day.

HAVE I HEALED MY ATTITUDE?

After practicing the above exercises, contemplate the following questions and write about your feelings in a journal.

1. Am I more conscious of the times I block my love essence as well as the times I extend it?

2. Am I more consciously aware of the love essence of others, especially those towards whom I feel conflict?

3. Have I become less fearful of my own thoughts and of the thoughts of others?

4. Has my sense of equanimity increased, particularly in stressful situations?

5. Is there any difference in how I experience my day on mornings that I meditate?

6. Do I now take time to recenter myself whenever I lose sight of my essence?

7. Has there been any noticeable shift in the quality of those relationships in which I have been experiencing conflict?

APPLYING THE PRINCIPLE IN SERVICE

This principle provides you as the facilitator with a philosophical context within which you can hold all of your supportive relationships. You are asked to hold yourself and others in your heart, with complete acceptance of the humanness and divinity of yourself and others. Stephen Levine states that with practice we "cultivate an openness of heart" and "we begin to experience the incredible power of this love. And we see that with all our imagined unworthiness and fear, with all our doubt and desire, it's hard to be loving all the time. But it's harder not to be loving."[4]

Love is the ever-present reality that constantly reveals itself to you in your facilitating work with others. The experience of self-love and love of others eventually becomes indistinguishable. Just as you are not capable of loving another person unless you love yourself, loving another person reflects back to you the experience of loving yourself.

As a facilitator, you have a responsibility to care for and nurture yourself physically, mentally, emotionally and spiritually so that you become increasingly aware of your love essence. You cannot be a source of love or strength unless you nurture that love and strength within yourself. As a facilitator, you cannot create a space in which others feel safe and comfortable unless you create being safe and comfortable with yourself. Others trust you when you trust yourself.

You must decide what disciplines best serve to nurture you physically, mentally, emotionally and spiritually. The discipline of daily meditation and contemplation is essential. Personally, I find it important to contemplate the meaning of a dream I had the night before, the dynamics of a current issue or a current quality I want to strengthen within myself. I strive to confront upsets as they occur rather than ignore or deny them. I spend much time in silence and monitor time spent with distractions.

As a facilitator, it is important for you to work on the union of work and play so that you begin to experience living your life fully each day. The words of Joseph Campbell serve to inspire us to seek the blissfulness of living:

> People say that what we're all seeking is a meaning for life. I don't think that's what we're really seeking. I think that what we're seeking is an experience of being alive, so that our life experiences on the purely physical plane will have resonances within our own innermost being and reality, so that we actually feel the rapture of being alive.[5]

Supporting others is one way in which the blissfulness of life can be experienced. As you open your heart, you become more alive and you begin to live life more fully.

HOW AM I DOING?

Periodically assess your progress in applying this principle in service to others. Note your concerns, questions and feelings in a journal.

1. How am I doing physically? Do I need to strengthen the care of my body?

2. How am I doing emotionally? Am I meeting my emotional needs?

3. How am I doing mentally? Do I need to strengthen my knowledge or expand my learning?

4. How am I doing spiritually? Do I need to strengthen my spiritual practice?

5. Am I more aware of my own self-love when I am serving others?

6. Am I seeing the love essence of the person I am supporting?

7. Do I more clearly see how being of service relates to living my life fully?

Chapter Six

𝒩 othing in life is to be feared.
It is only to be understood.

Marie Curie

Principle Two

HEALTH IS INNER PEACE. HEALING IS LETTING GO OF FEAR

BASIC TENETS

1. *Health is a state of being, a state of mind that is harmonious, active, flexible, alive and energized. Health, in this context, is not about the physical condition of the body.*

2. *The goal of health is inner peace.*

3. *Health is achieved through healing a fearful mind.*

4. *Healing is the process of removing obstacles to the goal of inner peace.*

5. *Fear with its many forms of expression— anger, guilt, jealousy, conflict, doubt, insecurity, confusion — is the obstacle to inner peace.*

6. *All physical and mental illness is viewed as an opportunity to heal the mind of its fears and therefore as an opportunity for spiritual growth.*

7. *There are only two emotions, love and fear.*

8. *The first step in letting go of fear is acknowledging that fear exists in one's mind and observing it.*

9. *The basis of all fear is the belief that one is separated from others and from the Divine Source.*

10. *Healing of the mind is usually a gradual process that occurs over time and that requires commitment, persistence and patience. At times, healing occurs instantaneously.*

THE PRINCIPLE'S MESSAGE

I grew up in a family whose philosophy was, "you don't have anything if you don't have your physical health." Like most families, health was defined primarily in terms of the functioning of the body. Our society as a whole focuses on the health of the body and fails to address how to develop and maintain a healthy mind and spirit. There is little education, preparation and guidance, for example, for those with the most influential and powerful role in life – that of a parent. As a result, families often have tremendous emotional struggles and problems, which accumulate over years and generations because they are never attended to.

In attitudinal healing, health is not about the physical condition of the body. Rather, health is defined as a state of being, a state of mind that is free of conflict, that is harmonious, active, flexible, alive and energized. In that state, a person is totally in the moment, engaged in living life fully and in a place of genuine emotional and spiritual strength to meet all situations.

One reaches the goal of health (inner peace) through the process of healing the mind. Healing is the process of removing the obstacles to the goal. Fear, in its various forms, is the obstacle to inner peace. Therefore, letting go of fear is the healing process. Releasing fear in its various forms is usually a gradual process, like the peeling of an onion. Layer upon layer of fear falls away until the core of our being, our essence, our inner peace, our health is uncovered.

In the context of attitudinal healing, therefore, all physical illness is viewed as an opportunity to heal the mind, an opportunity for spiritual growth. This view is compatible with that of renowned surgeon, Bernie

Siegel, who authored the bestseller *Love, Medicine, and Miracles* and who developed an innovative approach to supporting cancer patients. Siegel's approach, paraphrased, is:

1. Accept your illness so that constructive energy is available for your use. An attitude of resignation is destructive and allows the illness to run your life. Acceptance means you know the illness is there but rather than a burden, it is something you can handle.

2. View your illness as a source of psychological growth, an opportunity to replace what was lost with growth.

3. View your illness not as a judgement but as a positive redirection of your life towards something that you are supposed to be doing. This implies that all is really okay and that this new direction is intrinsically right for you.

4. See death or recurrence of illness as further opportunities for growth and not as failure. Staying alive is not the goal but rather enjoying and living in the present. We all at some time have to accept the inevitability of death.

5. Focus on self-love and peace of mind and the body will respond. Your body receives the messages of your mind and your immune system is strengthened. Focusing on your self-worth, believing in yourself, and seeing that you have something to give to the world is what creates a life that is lived fully.

6. Make peace of mind, acceptance and forgiveness your goal and not getting over your physical illness. See the illness as a problem you are having, as a fear. Learn about hope, love, acceptance, forgiveness and peace of mind, and the illness may go away in the process.

7. Realize that the only way to have immortality is to leave the gift of love behind. Loving is living.[1]

Often when a person first begins to work with physical or mental illness as an opportunity for spiritual growth, he has to address an underlying fear. This is a fear of letting go of fear, a fear of the unknown, a fear of what one will discover in the process. One has to have the stance of a spiritual warrior when bringing to the surface and releasing years of suppressed and denied fears. A spiritual warrior represents that part of ourself that is willing and able to confront emotional pain and has the fortitude and stamina to persist in the healing process to its completion, even if this takes many years.

Understanding the nature of the psyche is extremely important. One can think of the different floors and rooms of a house as representing the various levels and functions of the human psyche. The ground floor represents the conscious self, the upper floors the higher self and the basement the lower self. During our waking hours, we relate to others and are nurtured on the ground floor, represented by the living room and kitchen. The basement is used for storage for those things we rarely use, things we want to keep for future needs or things we have no further use for but don't want to throw away. The upstairs represents our higher selves, a place where we store prized belongings or where we dream our highest dreams. There are closets throughout the house, where additional items of various sorts are stored. What is visible in a house may be relatively little, compared to what is stored or put away. So it is with our psyche. We have a conscious self which operates in daily life, yet many aspects and memories are put away, some very hidden and forgotten for years, some which no longer have a use in our lives but are still very much a part of our inner reality.

I first met Anna, a fifty-year-old woman, in one of my workshops. She shared that she had been raised in an abusive family and had left at age twenty vowing never to return. At the same time Anna insisted that unlike others with traumatic backgrounds, she did not have any fears or problems. Other people had painful lives; hers was happy. She was a successful career woman with a loving husband and family. Her reason for coming to the workshop was merely to bring a friend who "really needed help."

After this initial workshop, however, Anna continued to come to the Institute for other workshops and courses. Finally, while enrolled in the facilitator training course, she began to stop pretending. Cautiously she began to open long-closed doors of memory and to acknowledge her fears, her troubled and impoverished childhood and to discard her pretense that she was fine and happy.

As she began to clean her "mental closets," Anna began cleaning her physical closets at home as well. Material goods had held great importance to her; she rarely threw anything away. Now Anna felt a particular urge to discard a twenty-five-year collection of Vogue dress patterns which she had stored in her basement.

Looking at her housecleaning symbolically, as if it were a dream, was a useful tool for Anna. The dress patterns represented her desire to appear totally together (her "old pattern" in life). They were stored in the basement of her subconscious with her repressed memories. As Anna decided to stop pretending life was okay when it was not, she was willing to discard her old patterns of being. Although she had physically left her family thirty years ago, the memories and patterns had been stored away unhealed.

Anna's healing process began to accelerate as she confronted her fears and released her pain. Being in the group allowed Anna to acknowledge that she was loved while she was going through this process and to acknowledge her own strength. Being in this loving, safe space gave Anna permission to face her painful past. She was, indeed, a spiritual warrior.

When releasing fears, it is important to have what I like to call a "life line" – someone in one's life who represents unconditional love and can mirror this back. For Anna, this life line was the training course group. One's life line can also be one's meditation or prayer life or one's participation in Alcoholics Anonymous or other support programs. A life line is whatever serves as a reminder of one's true essence when difficult times are experienced while releasing fears.

We experience fear because of our belief in our separation from God and from humankind. Whenever we have the thought or experience of separation, we feel guilty and believe we deserve punishment. Because we expect punishment, we feel unsafe and because we feel unsafe, we develop defenses (obstacles) in the form of aspects of fear. The cycle then repeats itself. Our fear creates an atmosphere of isolation and loneliness; we feel that we are victims of events around us. Without the fear, we would feel perfectly safe and at peace. This is why in order to experience inner peace we must let go of the fear by healing our sense of separation and restoring love as our true identity.

While working on this chapter, I was preparing for a second pilgrimage to Medjugorje, the village in Yugoslavia where an apparition of the Virgin Mary has been occurring since 1981. Our Lady has appeared throughout history and has been a messenger and guide in times of great conflict. Physical and spiritual healings are associated with her appearances.

Fra Jozo Zovko, former parish priest in Medjugorje, tells the story of two Italian women, both confined to wheelchairs, who came to Medjugorje in hopes of physical healing.

> The elder of the two women was healed. The younger, Manuela, remained in her wheel-chair.

The one who was healed returned home, delighted at being able to walk again; Manuela stayed behind to give thanks and praise to God. They had both come with the desire to be healed, and they were both healed. But healing is not only physical, it is something that takes place in the heart. Manuela was healed in her heart. Full of joy, she praised God for having come to her, for shedding light on the cross she carried, for showing her its value and meaning. She understood that from her wheelchair she could bring people spiritual solace, telling them about the love of God, about goodness, about the wisdom that patience can bring. Manuela took a far greater joy home in her heart than the woman who went home able to walk. The Church was grateful for both blessings. Deeply grateful.[2]

In telling this story, Fra Jozo shares his conviction that the true healing is an inner one. Our Lady's message in Medjugorje is peace, that peace which begins in the heart and extends outward. Since health is inner peace, healing begins within.

WHAT IS MY ATTITUDE?

Contemplate the following questions and write about your feelings in a journal.

1. Under what circumstances am I most aware of being fearful and to what do I attribute my fear?

2. What are the priorities in my life and to what extent do they include the health of my own mind?

3. What investment might I have in remaining fearful?

4. Under what circumstances do I feel emotionally safe?

5. Remembering that health is defined as peace of mind, how would I describe my health?

6. Am I willing to consider that the health of my own mind needs to be a priority in my life?

7. What distractions in my life serve to impede my working on the healing of my own mind?

PRACTICING THE PRINCIPLE

Select the exercises that best facilitate and support your healing process, writing your responses in a journal. You may want to prerecord the visualization exercises.

1. Draw a vertical line down the middle of a blank sheet of paper. At the top of the left half write the word FEAR. At the top of the right half write LOVE. Now for the next few minutes contrast these two emotions using any words, phrases or descriptions you wish. For example, you might write "darkness" under FEAR and "light" under LOVE or "fragmenting" under FEAR and "whole" under LOVE.

Set your paper aside, sit in a comfortable position and close your eyes.

Recall a fear that you presently have or one you have had in the past; it could also be a fear related to the future.

What color is your fear? What size is it? What shape does it have? How does it feel to touch it? Can you smell it? What is its temperature? What sound does it make?

Now, personify your fear in some way. What does it look like? An animal? An insect? A person? What are its features?

Look at this frightening thing or creature. Stand face to face. Be patient, have courage. Stay with the process; don't hide or turn away from your fear.

As you face your fear, ask what message it has for you. What does it want to say to you? Take a few minutes and talk with it; listen to its message.

Now, imagine the two of you transported to a most beautiful valley. The two of you find yourselves among grass, trees, flowers; you see a mountain. You feel safe in this place.

The two of you begin to walk up the mountain together, side by side. Walk slowly; take your time. If you can do so, hold the hand of your fear or hold your fear in some way. If you cannot seem to do this, allow your fear to walk or move in some way alongside you, as you both ascend the mountain.

You notice as you ascend that the air is becoming purer and purer and you welcome the silence of the heights and beautiful scenery. Remain aware of the presence of your personified fear beside you.

As the two of you climb, you begin to notice that the fear is slowly changing; it's becoming something else. It is gradually transforming; it may even totally transform.

You reach the top of the mountain and the sun shines down on the two of you. And, now you may still see yet another transformation of your fear. What has the fear become? Let it express its constructive side, its highest potential.

Slowly open your eyes and ask yourself these questions: What did I experience? What transformations occurred and what might this tell me? Did a transformation not occur or did I want to resist following the imagery?

If you did not experience a transformation of your fear, you may need to do the exercise again. You may be having difficulty recognizing and accepting your fear. You need to allow it to be what it is, in order for it to communicate with you and transform into its highest potential. If you negatively judge the fear or do not accept it as a part of yourself, its constructive side will not appear. The fear then may increase in intensity and move into the unconscious. Ferrucci describes this process in the following way:

> . . . any content of our psyche can be degraded (literally 'stepped down from its higher state'). Compassion can become self-pity, joy can become mania, peace can become inertia, humor can become

sarcasm, intelligence can become cunning, and so on. But the converse is also true: contents of consciousness can be elevated; self-pity becomes compassion, and so on. In fact, nothing is ever static in the life of the psyche. And the higher we rise, the closer we will be to unity. Conflict is among distortions – but there is no clash at the source. As Teilhard de Chardin puts it, everything that ascends, converges.[3]

2. A dialogue is a conversation between two people. As a healing tool, dialoguing allows you to have conversations with people or animals (living or dead), with emotions (your anger, your fear, etc.) or with objects (a tree, money, etc.). You can dialogue by visualizing the person, animal, emotion or object or by writing to them and then writing their response to you. Dialoguing provides an opportunity to express your thoughts and feelings. As importantly, it allows an opportunity to listen to the other's point of view. Before beginning a dialogue it is helpful to meditate for a few minutes and to ask for guidance in communicating with clarity and honesty.

Dialogue exercise:

Dialogue in a visualization or in a journal first with your child self, then your adolescent self and, finally, your adult self. Ask each of these selves if he or she has fears of loneliness, of intimacy, or if he or she fears an event may happen again. Ask about needs unfulfilled. Ask about rewards for keeping the fears. Ask if the fear relates to a need to forgive. Reassure and comfort your inner selves. You may also dialogue with the fear itself. Dialogue with each of your selves or with your fear until you have a sense of completion. You may want to return to a dialogue and continue it at a later time.

3. Sit in a comfortable position and close your eyes. Picture yourself standing face to face with your mother. Notice the nature of bondage that seems to bind the two of you together. This bondage may be in the form of ropes, chains or barriers.

Ask a wise Holy Being to join the two of you. This Being must be a figure representing total and unconditional love at its highest, such as the Christ.

Ask the Being to cut, break and dissolve the bondage that exists between your mother and yourself. See that you are now each free from the other.

As you continue to face your mother, ask the Being, "Bridge the gap between the love I needed and the love I got from my mother."

Visualize the Being, you and your mother all holding hands as the Being radiates total unconditional love through both you and your mother.

Visualize the Being walking between you and your mother in a beautiful, natural setting. If it feels comfortable to do so, the three of you may want to hold hands or embrace one another.

Complete the visualization in whatever way feels right for you. You may want to continue feeling the presence of the Being walking with the two of you or you may want the Being to now leave so that you and your mother can walk in love together. Or, you and your mother may want to converse with the Being or with each other.

Redo the process with your father. Then do it with any person in your life with whom you feel you have an unhealed relationship.

4. Close your eyes and visualize a person towards whom you feel fear, anger or conflict standing next to a blackboard.

Walk up to the blackboard and write all the resentments, upsets and feelings you have about this person. Be as complete with your list as you can.

Then erase the blackboard thoroughly so that the "slate is clean."

Face the person and say with genuine feeling, "I make a promise to you. I will no longer project onto you who or what I think you are. From now on, I want you to write who you really are on the board."

Observe if the person chooses to write any words; if not, let that be okay. Check back periodically throughout the days and weeks to see if the person has written anything.

Whenever you see or think of this person and you find yourself interpreting his behavior and becoming upset, recreate yourself erasing the blackboard, reaffirm your vow and see if you can visualize the person writing who he is on the board.

5. Draw a vertical line down the middle of a blank sheet of paper. On the left-hand side identify your range of fears by writing each of them in a simple statement. For example, you might write "I am afraid to speak in front of a group." Opposite this statement on the right-hand side of the paper, write a positive affirmation reflecting some quality or strength you can recall when in this particular situation. For example, you might write, "I value and appreciate my unique self." Or, you may write on the left, "I am afraid to drive on the freeway" and on the right, "I am alert and careful when I drive." The positive affirmations must reflect a belief you have about your strengths and which you can therefore call upon in the situation. Use these affirmations in the actual situations in which you experience yourself as fearful.

6. Say the following affirmations before you begin your day, returning to them throughout the day whenever you find yourself experiencing fear or conflict. This is an adaptation of a psychosynthesis dis-identification exercise suggested by Assagioli in his book *The Act of Will*.

> I have a body, but I am not my body. I am more than
> that.
> My body may be in different conditions of health or
> sickness.
> It may be rested or tired, but it is not my real "I."
> My body is my precious instrument of experience
> and of action, but it is not my self.
> I have a body, but I am not my body. I am more than
> that.
> I am the one who is aware.
>
> I have emotions, but I am more than my emotions.
> They are countless, contradictory, changing,
> And yet I know that I always remain I, my self,
> In a state of irritation or calm.

Since I can observe, understand and judge my
Emotions and then increasingly dominate, direct
And utilize them, it is evident that they are not my
    self.
I have emotions, but I am not my emotions. I am
    more than that.
I am the one who is aware.

I have an intellect, but I am more than my intellect.
It may be quiet or active.
It is capable of expanding, letting go of limiting
    beliefs and learning new attitudes.
It is an organ of knowledge in regard to the inner
    world as well as the outer. But it is not my self.
I have an intellect, but I am not my intellect. I am
    more than that.
I am the one who is aware.

I am a center of pure self-awareness.
I am a center of will,
Capable of mastering and directing all my energies:
Physical, emotional, mental and spiritual.
I am the one who is aware.
I am the self.[4]

As you use this process, you may want to change it to serve your own situation. For example, if you are having issues with your job, you could design an "I have a job, but I am not my job" statement fitting your job issues.

HAVE I HEALED MY ATTITUDE?

After practicing the above exercises, contemplate the following questions and write about your feelings in a journal.

1. Having affirmed that I am more than a body, emotions and intellect, am I experiencing less fear?

2. What is my definition of health now?

3. Am I more aware of my inner state when in a fearful situation and have my responses or reactions shifted in any way?

4. Do I see that the underlying fear in all situations relates to perceiving some form of separation?

5. Am I more willing to use tools and affirmations for releasing fear when it comes up in my life?

6. Do I notice any shift in my inner awareness when I am in situations that usually bring forth some form of fear for me?

7. Am I aware of incorporating more nurturing and care of my emotional and spiritual self in my life and do I see any shift in my physical well-being?

APPLYING THE PRINCIPLE IN SERVICE

Naturalist John Muir, who is known for studying and exploring nature by living in it for extended periods of time, told a wonderful story about Stickeen, a dog who used to accompany him on many of his outdoor adventures. The dog had an enduring and loyal relationship with Muir and he liked to join Muir even in the middle of storms and in treacherous country. This particular story occurred on a trek across glaciers in Alaska.

Muir discovered as night was falling that he and Stickeen faced an enormous crevasse which was passable only by a precarious ice-sliver bridge. Muir realized that there was no alternative but to cross the deep and broad chasm by walking the narrow ice-covered ledge.

Muir knew there was no way he could safely carry the dog across with him. With great remorse, he left the dog behind. Stickeen watched intently as Muir walked the ledge to safety. Muir looked back at the sad and lonely dog who loved him so much. At first the dog paced back and forth, as he deliberated whether to also walk across the ledge. It seemed an impossibility to Muir that the dog could make it. After much deliberation, the dog finally decided to walk across.

Safe at last, Muir said that he "ran and cried and barked and rolled about fairly hysterical in the sudden revulsion from the depth of despair to triumphant joy. I tried to catch him and pet him and tell him how good and brave he was, but he would not be caught. He ran round and round, swirling like autumn leaves in an eddy, lay down and rolled head over heels."[5]

This story is a reminder of how absolutely joyful and ecstatic it is to successfully face our fears, to walk through them and to make it to the other side. Muir writes that wherever he went, people begged to hear this inspirational story about the dog. He said that Stickeen had "enlarged my life," for "through him as through a window I have ever since been looking with deeper sympathy into all my fellow mortals."[6] I am sure this story speaks to many concerning their own challenges with fear and their desire to have the courage to "get to the other side."

The role of a facilitator is to support another's process of acknowledging fear, choosing what course of action to take, walking through the fear and then celebrating the successful walk. Like Stickeen, each of us has to find our own inner strength and commitment to make the walk and to make the choice independent of another. Muir could not make the choice for the dog. He could, however, be an example of the successful outcome of such a choice.

Love was the ultimate reason the dog made the decision to cross, the love that he and Muir had for one another. Two people in the context of love for one another as fellow humans can join together in the common purpose of transcending a fear. Your presence and experience, as a facilitator, is an assurance that such a walk is possible.

Because of the way this principle defines health, you may find it challenging to stay on purpose in the supportive process. Health is viewed as not of the body but of the mind. This does not mean that the body and its well-being are denied. It does mean that it is the mind that determines whether you or another are going to be peaceful or not peaceful, regardless of what is happening in the body. The body does not create inner peace, the mind does. As a facilitator, you need to support another within the context of this idea, focusing on the healing of attitudes and not the healing of the body.

You must remember that letting go of fear is usually a gradual process that occurs over time. You and the other each have your own pacing and your own way to release fear. In general, the steps of letting go of fear include:

Recognizing the fear

Engaging the Witness Self

Confronting the fear

Communicating with the fear

Being willing to have the fear released

Asking for healing of the conditions that brought the fear about

Opening to the presence of grace in the process

Staying with the process that unfolds

Acknowledging the progress made

When facilitating a person who is working through fears, it is important for you to remain a witness and not to become involved in the process. When someone shares a fear, it is easy to identify it as your own. If this happens during facilitation, the facilitator becomes part of the problem instead of part of its solution.

You, as a facilitator, need to be aware that your fears may differ in kind and nature from the fears of the person you are facilitating. For example, the person may have a fear of death but you may not, or you may have a fear of abandonment and the person may not. It is important not to project onto the other person what is true for you and assume it is true for him. You can also not assume that what works for one person in letting go of his fear will work for another. You can, however, assist someone in viewing fear as a teacher, as an opportunity to learn and to heal. Your most important function as a facilitator is to be fully present and to be a witness regarding another's fear.

Because identification with the fear can block its release, you also need to encourage the person to cultivate his Witness Self. From this viewpoint, the person can work with the fear without attachment. Use of the dis-identification exercises is helpful in cultivating the Witness Self.

HOW AM I DOING?

Periodically assess your progress in applying this principle in service to others. Note your concerns, questions and feelings in a journal.

1. Am I able to stay focused on the definition of health as used in this principle or do I move into the belief that health is only of the body?

2. Am I staying in my own Witness Self when I see someone in a state of fear?

3. Do I see clearly the many forms that fear takes?

4. When fear is triggered within myself, do I take responsibility for this by doing my own healing work?

5. Am I mindful of the pacing of the person being supported and am I trustful of that pacing as being right for him?

6. Am I free of interpretations and assumptions about the person and his process?

7. Am I careful to view fear as a teacher and not to judge myself or the other person for having fear?

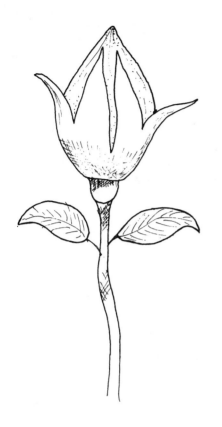

Chapter Seven

w e are so both and oneful
night cannot be so sky
sky cannot be so sunful
i am through you so i

e e cummings

Principle Three

GIVING AND
RECEIVING ARE
THE SAME

BASIC TENETS

1. *We are giving and receiving all the time whether we are conscious of it or not.*

2. *The thoughts we have and share, positive or negative, are strengthened in our minds and are communicated to the minds of others.*

3. *Throughout life, giving is essential to one's well-being.*

4. *The unity of giving-receiving needs to be recognized and nurtured throughout our lives.*

5. *Inherently, we have been given all that we need to live our lives meaningfully and fully.*

6. *To give without being open to the awareness of receiving leads to emotional fatigue, "burn-out" and lack of self-worth.*

7. *All that we give is given to ourselves; what we perceive in the outside world is a mirror of our inner state.*

8. *We must be willing to value ourselves and others enough to receive every kind and loving thought extended to us.*

9. *True giving is unconditional, having no expectations and needing no rewards.*

10. *We can decide what we want to give to others and we have the power and freedom to create that as a reality.*

THE PRINCIPLE'S MESSAGE

At one time I thought that giving was one thing and receiving quite the opposite. I had a rather "missionary" attitude in that I thought there were two groups of people in the world, those who were givers and those who received what the givers had to give. This obviously led to a "me/they" view in my relationships with family, friends and professional associates.

To separate giving from receiving and receiving from giving is unnatural and not nurturing to ourselves or others. By focusing on giving without simultaneously receiving, the messages one gives oneself and the other are: "I am strong, you are weak," "I've got the answers, you haven't," "You need help, I don't." As the giver in this instance, one immediately feels fearful because of the secret knowledge that one's own weaknesses, questions and helplessness might be exposed at any moment.

On the other hand, by focusing on receiving without simultaneously giving, one conveys to oneself and to the giver a message of powerlessness, helplessness and dependence. The receiver in this instance is always locked in the fear that the giver may leave and is obsessed with the secret knowledge that no other person can truly meet another's needs. The giver in this situation is weighed down by fears of exposure of his own weaknesses and often resents the receiver.

Both premises result in our not seeing or experiencing the inner strength in ourselves or others. We therefore do not feel nurtured by our relationships with others or feel cared for by ourselves.

A vivid demonstration of the simultaneity of giving and receiving recently occurred in a workshop. One of the exercises in this workshop involves participants facing one another for fifteen minutes and looking into one another's eyes, watching the thoughts of the mind and focusing on being with that person. This exercise provides an immediate opportunity to experience the simultaneity of giving and receiving. Within moments after this exercise began, two partners, Julia and David, both began sobbing. I had no idea what was happening but decided to let them be until the exercise was completed.

The story that the two people shared was this. David was a veteran of the Vietnam War and for twenty years he had been carrying great hatred for not only the Vietnamese but for all Asians. Julia, being Chinese, had carried self-hatred because of her deep resentment of her Asian heritage. Of course, by "accident" the two were paired with one another, although both admitted they tried to avoid it. At the moment of their facing one another there occurred an instant healing, David of his twenty years of hatred towards the Asians that Julia represented and Julia towards herself for being Oriental. In an instant of time, they simultaneously gave and received unconditional love to themselves and to each other.

As we grow throughout our childhood and teenage years, our giving-receiving balance needs to be continually nurtured and supported in order for us to become emotionally healthy as adults. The writings of Edgar Cayce repeatedly emphasize that from early in life, the child must be given opportunities to give by using his natural interests and abilities within the family and school. This means participation in the function and running of the family and school in a very practical and meaningful way, not as chores that need to be done but as an organization that works more harmoniously and effectively because of his unique contribution. In this way, the child receives nurturing and feedback as a valuable individual and begins developing a sense of self-worth and an understanding of community.

In today's world, home and school are structured in such a way that giving and receiving are presented as separate experiences. Children are expected to achieve, do their homework, play and do chores as if these were separate tasks, unrelated to purpose and meaning. Without real training and experience in how to do so, adults are expected to have a clear understanding of how to contribute and give to others. Lack of early opportunity to learn how to give and receive accounts for much of the unrest and uncertainty in our youth today, for it is this that gives an individual meaning and purpose for his life. If a child's natural joy in giving is nurtured, he will find the way to live his life fully as a teenager and as an adult rather than to look for life's meaning in drugs, money, material goods, achievement and sex.

Focusing on helping others without simultaneously working on oneself can lead to disillusionment and emotional fatigue and an imbalance of the giving and receiving cycle. This phenomenon often occurs when a person has unmet emotional needs and attempts to meet these needs through a relationship with a person needing assistance. An unhealed healer is one who gives in hopes of receiving what he needs. Therefore he does not give from the place of a true connection to an inner state of emotional and spiritual abundance.

Since what we are is what we give away, this principle asks that we become aware of our inner state. Our thoughts create energy that define what we are and that energy can be sensed by others. We are always giving what we are to others and on some level, they identify what it is we are giving.

Have you ever had the experience of walking into a room filled with people and sensing whether or not you are welcome? If you feel welcomed, the people in the room are having thoughts and feelings of acceptance and openness. Provided you are open to this energy, you will find yourself reciprocating and willingly joining the group. The people not only give this welcoming state, but they strengthen that energy within themselves. They therefore receive for themselves what they have given, i.e., welcome, openness and acceptance.

On one level you experience being given this welcoming by them. On another level, your inner awareness of acceptance has been triggered so you are in the state of acceptance also. You *become* acceptance and thus receive it. To share strengthens what we give and so we receive what we give in this way. To share our state of acceptance strengthens that state inside of us and so we receive what we give.

If you imagine the infinity sign (∞) as representing this concept, you will notice that the energy moves in a loop. What is given returns to the place it was given from. That is how this principle works.

I remember experimenting with this concept in my late teens and early twenties when I worked as a long distance telephone operator while going to college. If I had a disgruntled customer I tended to become disgruntled myself. On the other hand, if I communicated patience and helpfulness, the customer would become pleasant. If I became disgruntled when the customer was pleasant, the customer would soon become irritable. I discovered I could literally get back the state of mind I was conveying.

Since we are giving all the time, we might as well be responsible about it and decide what it is that we want to put out into the world. In his autobiography, Benjamin Franklin writes about his desire to improve his relationships and communications with others and to correct what he considered to be faulty thinking. He found that he felt better emotionally and spiritually and his relationships went more smoothly when he practiced what he researched to be the necessary twelve "virtues." These included temperance, silence, order, resolution, frugality, industry, sincerity, justice, moderation, cleanliness, tranquility and chastity. When he was subsequently told of his pride, he added humility, to make the list thirteen. Franklin devised a simple system of recording his success and failures in practicing these virtues in his relationships until they became a natural "habit."[1]

Reading about the life of Mother Teresa, one discovers that because she is in a state of inner peace, fearlessness and wisdom gained through experience, she communicates those qualities to all who come in contact with her.[2] Brother Lawrence, Peace Pilgrim and St. Francis are also models of this principle applied to its highest.[3] Who is to say that we all can't someday become like them by receiving what they have given us through their example?

What we give is what we get back. Often people coming for facilitation are very focused on the ways in which the world is not meeting their needs. As long as they see themselves as victims of the circumstances around them, they do not see that the world is merely giving back what they have given.

When Joe first came to see me, he described how people ignored him, refused him support and help and rejected him. As he learned to examine his own attitude, he began to see how he excluded and rejected others and withheld his support and help from them. He was getting back what he was giving.

Whenever we find ourselves blaming people or circumstances for our problems, we must look to see how we are giving what we are blaming "them" for. Seeing the worst instead of the best in a person is a mirror of what we see in ourselves. When you see the worst in yourself, that is what you will see in others. When you see the best in yourself, that is what will be mirrored back to you.

WHAT IS MY ATTITUDE?

Contemplate the following questions and write about your feelings in a journal.

1. Do I see giving and receiving as two separate, disconnected experiences or as one unified experience?

2. Do I feel I give more than I receive or receive more than I give?

3. What quality do I really want to experience in my inner reality and in my life? Am I doing anything to create this quality?

4. Even if I do not currently have this quality and have trouble imagining having it, can I view this quality as a possibility?

5. In what physical, emotional, mental and spiritual areas do I experience lack right now in my life?

6. In what physical, emotional, mental and spiritual areas do I experience abundance right now in my life?

7. How aware am I of the nature of my thoughts and to what extent am I aware of their effect on others?

PRACTICING THE PRINCIPLE

Select the exercises that best facilitate and support your healing process, writing your responses in a journal. You may want to prerecord the visualization exercises.

1. Make a list of those qualities that you would like to cultivate and manifest in your life by living them, being them and expressing them. Be selective, making the list of all those qualities you feel are essential to bring harmony and joy into your life. For now limit the list to five or six qualities. Prioritize the list by reflecting on which qualities you feel are most critical for you to have and express right now in your life.

Select the first quality and write it at the top of a blank page, perhaps in your journal. Contemplate the quality, asking yourself these questions. What does it mean to me? How would I define it? What does it feel like to experience this quality? When have I experienced it? In what situations? In what situations now would I like to express it? What keeps me from doing that? How might I remind myself to practice this quality?

On a personal calendar, write the first letter of that quality near the number designated for every day in one week. When you look at your calendar you will be reminded of your need to express that quality. You may want to put other reminders in your home and work environment. These reminders may take the form of the word itself, an affirmation or a symbol. You may want to do specific imageries or meditations that strengthen your understanding and expression of this quality. Periodically contemplating the quality is especially helpful.

At the end of each day as you near sleep, reflect upon your awareness and practice of this quality throughout the day. Be careful not to judge yourself but to merely take an inventory of how vigilant you were throughout the day. Acknowledge those times you found yourself practicing that quality and observe the times that you didn't.

Depending on what feels appropriate, you might work on one quality for more than a week or you may want to select the second quality for the second week. This exercise can be adapted to your unique needs. Benjamin Franklin, who is our inspiration for this exercise, worked on one quality a week and after completing his list of thirteen qualities, he began over again, so that the exercise continued throughout the year. He considered the exercise complete when he was successful in practicing that quality effortlessly and automatically, so that it was a part of his being, a "habit." When I used this technique to learn how to practice equanimity in my life, I found that I practiced this quality for a full year before it became a part of myself! I periodically do a refresher exercise, when I notice my equanimity has "weakened."

2. Either ask someone to join you in this exercise or do it by looking at your face in a mirror. If you do it with someone, sit across from them, knee to knee but not touching. For ten to fifteen minutes look into each other's eyes, not in a staring way but to be present with the person. Observe your thoughts. Watch them and try not to hold on to them. As you are with this person, be aware of what it is you are giving or sending and of what you are receiving. Ask yourself if you are receiving what you are sending.

After you finish looking into one another's eyes, share your experience, focusing on what was given and received by each of you.

If you do this exercise in front of the mirror, look into your eyes and become aware of your thoughts about who you are, what you are communicating, what you are sending and receiving from the person in the mirror. You may want to journal your thoughts regarding this exercise in order to acknowledge your experience.

3. Make a list of physical, emotional, mental or spiritual qualities that you feel you have to give to others. For example, you might list endurance, physical beauty, kindness, gentleness, curiosity, compas-

sion and so forth. Observe your inner thoughts as you compile this list, noting what memories or thoughts come to your mind. Note if you found it difficult to think of qualities to add to the list or if you evaluated your giving with thoughts about limitations you set on it.

Now make a list of physical, emotional, mental or spiritual qualities that you have been given, such as good health, stamina, beautiful eyes, intelligence, responsibility, forgiveness and so forth. Again, observe your thoughts and considerations as you write your list.

When you have completed both lists, ask yourself these questions: Are my lists made up of the same or different qualities? How long or short are the lists? What list seemed the hardest to write and what might that be saying to me? Was I aware of any conditions I placed on my willingness to acknowledge what I have to give and/or what I have been given?

The lists will change if you periodically write them. At first you may only be able to acknowledge a few qualities but over time, as you heal and grow, you will find your lists will grow and change.

4. Experiment with shifting your inner thoughts to those of peace and well-being when you find yourself in a stressful situation, focusing on bringing the energy of peace to the situation rather than fear. Observe how this begins to change your perception of a situation.

5. At the end of every day, record and acknowledge what you have given throughout the day and what you have received that has nurtured you.

HAVE I HEALED MY ATTITUDE?

After practicing the above exercises, contemplate the following questions and write about your feelings in a journal.

1. Am I more aware of my thoughts and am I better able to observe them?

2. Am I more receptive to the acknowledgements that others express or give to me?

3. Am I more willing to acknowledge myself for the progress I am making in my personal growth?

4. Do I see that I am bringing my own inner state to any stressful situation and that I can choose what I want to bring?

5. Have I become more conscious about what I contribute to the lives of others and have I made any new decisions about what it is I truly want to give to others?

6. Am I placing myself in situations where I have an opportunity to give?

7. Is my giving more unconditional and without expectations?

APPLYING THE PRINCIPLE IN SERVICE

This principle asks that as a supporter of others, you be responsible for your own state of mind, knowing that these thoughts affect not only yourself but others.

Your primary goal as a facilitator is to be in a state of being that reflects nonjudgement, compassion and wisdom, and to create a safe space where feelings and concerns can be acknowledged. A facilitator creates a space where as few thoughts as possible are projected outward.

I once counseled a woman, Lacey, who was so sensitive to my thoughts that she could tell at any moment what I was thinking! She requested that I be with her in an unconditional, loving way. She specifically asked that I not interfere with her process, not comment on it, not interpret it and not advise her. She asked that I not even think about her process. Lacey knew the moment my mind started thinking any thoughts whatsoever and would question why I wasn't being with her unconditionally.

I soon recognized that the principle GIVING AND RECEIVING ARE THE SAME was operating fully in our relationship. I gave her the gift of an experience of unconditional love which she felt she had never had in her life. Lacey taught me how to be in and maintain a healing presence, namely a state of unconditional acceptance, with no thoughts and therefore no judgements. It took great discipline for me to achieve this and to this day I know she gave me a great gift, one that endlessly serves me.

This principle asks that, as a facilitator, you focus on your own healing and aspire to hold a state of total and unconditional love. Holding in your mind the ideal of Mother Teresa, Brother Lawrence or Peace Pilgrim is helpful. Those of us providing support need role models, teachers who demonstrate by who they are what it truly means to be of service.

It is your responsibility as a facilitator to be vigilant and watchful of what it is you are receiving and giving. In this way, the relationship is a partnership, a mutual opportunity to learn and grow. Acknowledging oneself and the other person for these gifts is important and should be part of the work together.

This principle focuses on the quality of the relationship rather than on the technique. Each of you can join in the exploration of your own experiences and each can be acknowledged and nurtured.

HOW AM I DOING?

Periodically assess your progress in applying this principle in service to others. Note your concerns, questions and feelings in a journal.

1. What quality did I communicate to the person when I was with him?

2. Was I aware of receiving a gift from the person and if so, what was it?

3. How quiet was my mind?

4. Did I feel any lack or scarcity when I was with the person?

5. What did the person reflect back to me that gave me an idea about what I was communicating?

6. Did I have any expectations of rewards from supporting the person?

7. What personal growth do I feel I gained from the experience of supporting someone and what would I do differently the next time?

Chapter Eight

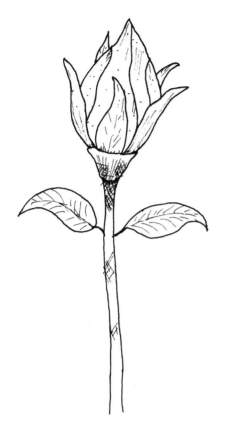

I *was regretting the past*
and fearing the future.

Suddenly my Lord was speaking:
"My Name is I AM."
                            He paused.
I waited. He continued:

"When you live in the past,
with its mistakes and regrets,
it is hard. I am not there.
My Name is not I WAS.

"When you live in the future,
with its problems and fears,
it is hard. I am not there.
My Name is not I WILL BE.

"When you live in this moment,
it is not hard. I am here.
My Name is I AM."[1]

Helen Mallicoat

Principle Four

WE CAN LET GO OF THE PAST AND OF THE FUTURE

BASIC TENETS

1. *To let go of the past and of the future means to open fully to the gift of the present moment.*

2. *When we say we are speaking from our past experience, we are speaking from internalized perceptions of our past experiences.*

3. *Ridding ourselves of past perceptions is a prerequisite to being fully in the present.*

4. *The past is recreated in the present when we bring our past perceptions into our present experience. In this way we are living in the past while acting in the present.*

5. *Anytime we find ourselves reacting instead of acting, we are bringing our past perceptions into the present.*

6. *Perceptions of our experience become firmly established as patterns in the psyche during our childhood. This conditioning is passed on unconsciously from generation to generation.*

7. *As adults we project our past out onto the world. We then perceive what we have projected as coming from outside us.*

8. *Being accountable for our projections is the first step to healing our perceptions. Healing our internalized perceptions allows us to see ourselves and others differently.*

9. *We step out of the present moment when we bring fears or expectations of the future into the present.*

10. *The future is created by the present. To create a peaceful future, we create a peaceful present. The present moment is continuously becoming the future.*

THE PRINCIPLE'S MESSAGE

To let go of the past one must first be willing to acknowledge that the past is defined by perceptions of our experiences. Most of these perceptions are not conscious. How our parents related to us throughout childhood and how we internalized the dynamics of this relationship lives in our unconscious. This pool of knowledge represents the primary programming from which we live as an adult. It is our past. The adult functions in the present from the reference of his inner child. As long as he does not acknowledge and heal his childhood sufferings, he will unconsciously pass them on to the next generation.

The noted Swiss psychoanalyst Alice Miller has clarified the relationship between the stored childhood in our psyches and our adult selves. Miller describes the vicious cycle within the psyche – what was done to us becomes what we do to others. Unless our inner child is healed, we parent from that wounded inner child and pass on the wounds to our children. Miller shows how we combat our own internalized parents through our own children, stating that "they (parents) are helpless when it comes to understanding their child so long as they must keep the sufferings of their own childhood at an emotional distance."[2]

Charles Whitfield, a physician who specializes in addictions and childhood abuse, states that when the inner child is wounded we as adults "live our lives from a victim stance, and experience difficulties in resolving emotional traumas. The gradual accumulation of unfinished mental and emotional business can lead to chronic anxiety, fear, confusion, emptiness and unhappiness."[3]

Healing the wounded inner child is an essential step towards letting go of the past. Visualizing one's inner child, one can reassure and comfort him, unconditionally love him and accept his feelings and his individuality. One can reparent the inner child by giving him in the present what he needed in the past – emotionally, physically and spiritually. Our adult self can bridge this gap for our wounded inner child. Once this gap has been bridged and healing of the inner child occurs, the parent will clearly see the uniqueness of his own children and will provide them with a nurturing and healthy emotional environment within which to "become." The pattern of the parent's emotional wounds will not be projected onto the children and the generational cycle will be broken.

Alice Miller writes that she:

> . . . can imagine that someday we will regard our children not as creatures to manipulate or to change but rather as messengers from a world we once deeply knew, but which we have long since forgotten who can reveal to us more about the true secrets of life, and also our own lives, than our parents were ever able to. We do not need to be told whether to be strict or permissive with our children. What we do need is to have respect for their needs, their feelings, and their individuality, as well as for our own.[4]

What about the adult who acknowledges his inner wounded child but who is in the process of raising his children or who has teenagers or adult children? What about the adult who now realizes he has been expressing himself from the place of the inner wounded child? How can an adult heal his internalized destructive parenting patterns and live more fully in the present? The intention of this discussion is not to make parents and other adults feel guilty or to foster feelings of helplessness and hopelessness about how they have been parented or how they parent. To the contrary, the intent is to demonstrate the possibility of healing the inner child and through that, healing one's parent/child relationships.

As an adult, healing the wounded inner child takes place where the emotional and spiritual wounds reside, in the unconscious. It takes place in the level of the unconscious where we relate meaningfully to one another, the level of our universal connectedness. At this level all minds are joined for a common spiritual purpose, that of healing our perceptions, healing our minds. At this level we are able to acknowledge the bond we all share, the bond of being a human being. This level acknowledges that regardless of what anyone has said or done, we want to be free of the bondage of guilt. We want to reconnect to the Divine Source, the Higher Power. We want to be forgiven and we want to forgive because not doing so keeps us imprisoned in fears and in the past.

Naomi, a woman in her early seventies, came to one of the Institute's workshops because, in her words, "I need to attend to some important matters regarding my children before it's too late – before I die." Naomi had three adult sons, none of whom she had seen very often over the past several years. Following a bitter divorce from her husband, her sons had shifted their support and loyalty to their father's point of view. They had all but stopped communicating with their mother. Naomi felt profound grief about the estrangement. She had deep regrets about the early homelife of her sons and the role she had played in creating their present resentment of her. And, as she said, "I don't know what to do and I don't know how much longer I will be here to do it."

I asked Naomi to select men in the workshop to roleplay her sons and her former husband. I had all five of them sit in a circle as though they were together once again. I asked Naomi to first give a brief biographical sketch of each family member, simply stating facts concerning his name, age, work, residence, marital status, children and significant life events like severe illnesses, accidents and crises. I asked that she see the roleplayers as her sons and former husband, addressing each by name and always using the "you" pronoun. One at a time, she was asked to face each family member and, looking into his eyes, express the unspoken feelings held in her heart about him. She was not to speak at the personality level of accusations or justifications but at the level of previously undelivered and unshared thoughts and feelings about their relationship and events she regretted or appreciated.

The roleplayers were asked to also move into their heart consciousness, look into Naomi's eyes and listen with full attention and openness, truly "hearing" her. After Naomi felt complete with her communication with each family member, he was to respond to her, expressing his feelings, again not at the accusatory level but at the level of understanding. This often included an explanation of how he felt about his life when growing up and how he feels about his relationship with her now. Naomi and the family members were asked to stop only when they felt complete with their communications.

At the completion of this very moving exercise, Naomi looked radiant. She literally glowed with joy and relief for having delivered these important messages to her sons and husband.

On the Monday after the workshop, Naomi called with great excitement. That very morning she had received a phone call from her three sons! They expressed the desire to see her and to renew their relationship. Naomi, of course, was ecstatic. Their active healing work could now begin and as Naomi said, "And so now, when the time comes, I shall die happy and at peace."

One might think that Naomi's call from her sons the day after this exercise might be explained logically – her sons had been thinking about her and it just happened to be on that particular Monday that they decided to call. I think what happened cannot be explained by "logic," but was an expression of healing that occurs at the universal level of the unconscious, at the level where we are all meaningfully connected. Jung places meaningful universal connectedness in the collective unconscious and calls it synchronicity. The phone call from Naomi's sons was a synchronistic event. (Synchronicity is discussed in detail in Chapter Thirteen.)

I have seen the healing effects of this particular roleplay exercise many times. Sometimes it gets played out in reality as with Naomi and her sons. Other times, there are no external events that occur, but one's inner reality noticeably shifts and one feels lighter and experiences relief and calmness about the troubled relationship. Even if Naomi's sons had not called, her internalized relationship with them would have been healed. She was blessed to have her outer relationship healed, too.

To hear and to be heard at the level of heart consciousness is tremendously healing for the wounded psyche because it puts the heart and the mind back in alignment. Many of our emotional wounds stemming from childhood relate to events and experiences in which we either were not heard or did not feel emotionally or physically safe to be heard. Our heart moves out of alignment with our mind. We use our mind to defend, protect, justify or accuse and we close our heart to further hurt. Sometimes we need to do this as a child to survive psychologically; developmentally we do not have the necessary emotional tools to do otherwise and we are too young to physically leave the hurtful situation. It is not "wrong" to have done this; however, in our adult life continuing this pattern restricts our psychological and spiritual growth.

When we empty out a wounding experience and replace it with a healing one, we reestablish the heart-mind connection. The heart is once again open and in communication with the mind; they are in relationship. What we think and how we feel are united in purpose. The psyche is healthy whenever its conscious and unconscious are in communication, whenever the heart and mind are in balance.

Because minds are joined, the healing of one mind affects the minds of others. When one frees oneself and another from the bondage of guilt, both "know" what has happened at a meaningful and unconscious level. At an unconscious level, Naomi's sons "heard" her. Because of the genuineness of her communications, Naomi was able to release her sons from the bondage of her guilt. The past was released. Old patterns of relating were broken. In the present moment, her heart and mind came into alignment and healing occurred.

Another aspect of this principle is the concept of the internalization of experience. When we experience something, it is our perception of that experience that we store and not the experience itself. This explains why people can see the same event but remember it differently. As part of my own healing process, I checked my perceptions about some of the events that occurred in our childhood with my siblings. I was surprised to discover that they had perceived many of the events quite differently than I had.

From early childhood, we typically store our perceptions of the events we experience. These perceptions, once internalized, color and shade our inner reality. In the healing of the psyche, it is not the event that needs to be healed but our internalized perception of the event. If we do not heal our perceptions we will continue to make decisions based on them and therefore continually reexperience and reinforce our unhealed perceptions. For example, most of us have internalized what transactional analysis refers to as the "critical parent." If we do not heal this "critical parent," it continues to criticize us. In an attempt to combat this internalized inner parent, we become that role ourselves and criticize others. A critical parent does not have to be physically present in our life for us to engage in this pattern.

From these past experiences we develop expectations about how the future "should" be. These expectations are learned through our perceptions of life as we grow up and through whatever value system our particular family and society have taught us. We make life choices based on these early lessons, often negating our own inclinations and inner guidance to do so.

Part of the existential crisis of middle age is the recognition that our expectations are not being fulfilled – the foundation for our life choices is faulty and there is little time left for the future. Discovering that our expectations have not been and probably will not be met can lead us to despair, anger and depression.

Many men who have second families in middle age comment that they are able to enjoy their children so much more because they are no longer so involved in "getting somewhere." Now they can just *be*. As long as we are intent on the future, we are also fixed in the past and we are missing the present. As someone wisely said, "Life is a journey, not a destination."

Staying in the present moment involves being honest with ourselves about what we want to experience and honoring our own choices. Life is change; we can resist it or we can flow with it.

Whatever we create in the present is automatically transferred into the future. If we want a peaceful future, we create a peaceful present. If we want to break old patterns of perception so we are free of them in the future, we break them in the present.

Letting go of the future does not mean we are not accountable for creating a safe and nurturing future for the planet or that we don't plan a vacation or have the car checked before a long trip. It does mean that we stay open to the moment and the gifts of the unexpected. Naomi, by healing her past perceptions in the present moment of the workshop, created a beautiful future event, a healing with her sons.

WHAT IS MY ATTITUDE?

Contemplate the following questions and write about your feelings in a journal.

1. Am I aware of any present perceptions that have their roots in my childhood?

2. How would I describe my internalized mother? My internalized father?

3. Am I aware of any past perceptions that I have released?

4. Are there patterns in my relationships with others that I seem to be repeating?

5. What portion of my day seems to be spent in reacting to situations or people?

6. Does it seem difficult or easy to be accountable for my projections?

7. Do I seem to be future-oriented and if so, how does this manifest in my life?

PRACTICING THE PRINCIPLE

Select the exercises that best facilitate and support your healing process, writing your responses in a journal. You may want to prerecord the visualization exercises.

1. Write a biography of your mother from her viewpoint, using the pronoun "I." For example, "I was the second born in a family of four children. I was born in the year 1929 and was named after my father's sister. My parents had both emigrated to Canada from Russia and had met on the boat coming over. . . ."

Be as complete as you can, including basic facts about your mother's life as well as what you imagine were her feelings, dreams, joys and sorrows, beliefs, successes and disappointments. Write her life up to and including her present age and life situation. If she has died, complete the biography with her perspective from the "other side," including what she feels now looking back over her life. If you did not know your mother or she died in your childhood, first write the biography as you imagine her life to be and then write the biography of the woman who played the mother role.

Once you have finished, read through the biography carefully, identifying those events and emotional patterns that match those you have observed in your own life. If you find instances in which you purposely have done the opposite of your mother, examine if in fact the same result has occurred. For example, if you felt your mother was too strict, have you gone to the other extreme and either lived your adult life with no boundaries or raised your children with few limits? The behavior may be different but the issue may be the same, that of not knowing how to foster a healthy balance between setting boundaries and no boundaries.

Do the same exercise with your father or the man that served in that role for you.

Reflect on what you wish to do with the knowledge of these patterns. Ask yourself these questions: Can I claim these patterns as my own? Do I want to keep them? Shift my perception of them? Make a renewed commitment to my own inner healing process? Can I use this knowledge as a guide for my own process? Can I look at these patterns from my Witness Self? Can I look at them without guilt, as a learning opportunity and as a gift to humanity?

2. Select someone with whom you have some undelivered communications. In your journal, write a letter to that person from your heart consciousness, expressing those feelings and thoughts you have been unable to share with him or her. Go beyond the personality level of accusation and justification; reach into your own pain and find the greater truth and the truer issue. Perhaps it was not honestly telling the person of your own pain or of your own limitations. Perhaps it was not saying goodbye to someone before he died. Perhaps it was not expressing your appreciation and gratitude. Whatever the undelivered communication, it needs to be genuine and heart-centered. Write until you feel complete.

Then write a letter from that person to yourself. Imagine that this person knows that if you receive this previously undelivered communication, your emotional and spiritual well-being will be enhanced. Write everything this person would want to share with you from his heart if he could do so. Write from his point of view, how he experienced his life and his emotions. Write until you feel complete. To do this portion of the exercise, open your heart to the possibility that the person has within him the ability to communicate at this level.

3. In silence, project your inner child outward so he is standing in front of you. Notice his age and his demeanor. Reassure the child that you, the adult, will protect, nourish and love him. Ask him what he needs and answer these needs appropriately. Ask him if he needs to understand anything in the past, and provide the explanations. Listen closely to his fears and joys; accept him as he is. Hug the child, saying, "I love you just the way you are."

Do this exercise daily, allowing the imagery to have a life of its own. The inner child will guide you as to how you can best help him. Do not be afraid to parent him but honor his own pacing. Moving too quickly can result in the wounded inner child becoming more fearful and withdrawing further. Remember, the inner child does trust you, the adult, for you have not left him. You have kept him within you all these years. The two of you did make it – you did survive. You are still here, together.

4. Make a list of the physical, mental, emotional and spiritual goals you would like to manifest in your life within the next five years. Set the list aside.

Now make a list of the physical, mental, emotional and spiritual goals you would like to manifest in your life today, right now, this moment.

Compare your two lists. Ask yourself these questions: Do I see any parallels between the two lists? How do I feel about manifesting what is on my today's list, today? Can I do it? Just for today?

HAVE I HEALED MY ATTITUDE?

After practicing the above exercises, contemplate the following questions and write about your feelings in a journal.

1. Can I more easily acknowledge that my reactions in the present stem from my past perceptions?

2. Can I live my day more easily as a series of moments and not yield to thoughts of the past or future?

3. Am I more aware of how I express myself coming from my internalized parents and more able to consciously make another choice of expression?

4. Is my inner child more content and playful? Does he feel he can trust me and that I am there for him emotionally and spiritually?

5. Do I experience any shift in my perception of the persons I have delivered undelivered communications to in my private journal?

6. Do I feel more empowered in the present?

7. Am I more aware of speaking from my heart whenever a situation calls for it and it is appropriate to do so? Do my heart and mind feel more in alignment?

APPLYING THE PRINCIPLE IN SERVICE

Because healing past perceptions relates closely to healing the wounded inner child, you, as the facilitator, need to educate yourself about the concept of the inner child. The writings of Carl Jung, Alice Miller, Charles Whitfield and Ira Progoff are very helpful. The best teacher, however, is your own personal work with your wounded inner child. For most people, healing the child within is an ongoing process.

Your personal practice of speaking from the heart is a necessary prerequisite to recommending it to the person you are facilitating. When you are supporting someone who cannot open his heart to a hurtful relationship, explain to him what it means to communicate from the consciousness of the heart and share an example from your own life. Questions that may facilitate communicating from heart consciousness are: "What would you say to this person from your heart if you knew you had his full attention and that he were really hearing you? What do you really want him to hear? What do you want him to know? What do you need from him? What is it you need to hear him say to you?"

The facilitator models letting go of the past and of the future by being fully in the present moment. Maintaining good eye contact will support you in doing this. Inner guidance will come more easily for you when you are in the present. Using your Witness Self, observe when your thoughts go to the past or future and when you feel "not present." You can gently let the thoughts go and bring your attention back to the person.

Being emotionally and spiritually present for someone allows you to experience healing. To do this, you must be in the present moment. You will also experience healing in such a moment. Anytime you are fully in the present, you are emotionally and spiritually nurtured as well as nurturing. It is when you are in the present that you are experiencing your closest connection to the Divine Source.

How reality is perceived is a reflection of each person's unique inner system of perceptions. One perceives interactions in different ways depending on one's own inner state and what one projects onto the other person. A facilitator needs to be aware of these differences in perception and projection. For example, what you perceive may be different from the perceptions of the person you are supporting. Or, how the person perceives his experience may not match your perception. Asking for clarification of perceptions is important so that assumptions are not made and projections are lessened. A supportive space is hopefully created that contains as few assumptions and projections as possible.

HOW AM I DOING?

Periodically assess your progress in applying this principle in service to others. Note your concerns, questions and feelings in a journal.

1. Am I more able to be emotionally and spiritually present for the person I am supporting?

2. Is it easier to bring my mind back to the present when its attention goes to the past or the future?

3. Am I more aware of speaking from my heart consciousness when I am with a person?

4. Do my heart and mind feel more in alignment when I am facilitating?

5. Am I more confident about the clarity of my inner guidance when I am supporting someone?

6. Do I willingly check my assumptions and perceptions with the person I am supporting?

7. Am I aware of my own internalized critical parent? Do I make use of this awareness by doing further healing work with my own inner child?

Chapter Nine

He is everywhere.
He is the entire universe.
Through Him and Him only,
    you accomplish everything.
Abandon the pride of doership.
Don't carry that weight on your
    head.

Swami Muktanada

Principle Five

NOW IS THE ONLY TIME THERE IS AND EACH INSTANT IS FOR GIVING

BASIC TENETS

1. *To live life fully is to live every moment to its fullest.*

2. *Our inner strength is found in the moment; we disconnect from this strength when we separate ourselves from the moment and move into past or future thoughts.*

3. *Healing takes place in the present moment; when we join with someone in the moment, we create a space for healing to occur.*

4. *The Divine Source gives us guidance in the timelessness of the moment; the Universe, therefore, is speaking and guiding us every moment, all of the time.*

5. *In every moment we have everything we need in our human experience.*

6. *We can use time as a learning tool in our healing process.*

7. *Our natural state is to give every moment; we cannot stop giving but we can decide what it is we want to give.*

8. *When we give in the moment, we are renewed and revitalized; in that moment we are also being given to, we are receiving.*

9. *Giving is an intuitive, selfless action which has no expectations except to be loving.*

10. *We strengthen our ability to be in the intuitive moment through contemplation, meditation and prayer.*

THE PRINCIPLE'S MESSAGE

Because this principle states that we have the opportunity to give every instant of our lives, it specifically addresses the topic of being of service to others. As discussed earlier, being of service within the context of attitudinal healing means serving others through the example of our lives, through the state of our being and through the expression of love in action. There are nine attributes to being of service when viewed in this way – constancy, deliberateness, love, wisdom, extension, reciprocity, empowerment, multiplicity of form and individuality (see Chapter Four). These attributes account for the extraordinary variety of ways one can serve humanity and planet earth with a sense of vitality and enthusiasm.

Viewing living as a dynamic and vital opportunity to give in every moment of our lives, Joel Goldsmith, a gifted teacher, healer and author writes: "There is no other reason for staying on earth than the opportunity to love, and anybody who has experienced this knows that there is no joy like loving; no joy like sharing, bestowing, understanding, and giving, all of which are but other names of love."[1] As Goldsmith's quote indicates, living on earth is a dynamic process, one that is alive, vital, moving and joyous. Life gives us opportunities to love and give; opportunities to love and give, give us life. When we fail to view life in this way, we become depressed, withdrawn and disconnected from our purpose for being on earth.

Everyone loved Kent. He was a star athlete, a good student and a natural leader. For four years we elected him president of our high school class. He had a mysterious and charismatic way about him and one couldn't help but love him and want to be around him. Kent was offered numerous college scholarships when he graduated from high school. I thought for sure I would see his name in print someday as a leader of a great humanitarian cause. Kent married the month after high school graduation and became a farmer. Within months, he became severely depressed and stopped all outside contact. Now, thirty-five years after high school graduation, he lives as he has for many years, alone and isolated on his farm.

Kent's life is an example of the dynamic relationship between living and giving. His life shows us how closely this relationship relates to one's emotional and spiritual health. For a period of time, Kent seemed to be able to live life fully and accept the many opportunities he was given to serve. He served through his state of being, his example and his actions. He received much acknowledgement and he was loved by many. However, as Kent's adult life demonstrates, his inner life was obviously troubled. A person can be loved by millions and still be miserable. Because of unresolved pain, Kent withdrew. He no longer accepted opportunities to give. He actively stopped giving. Kent did continue to serve others in an indirect way, however, through the example of his life. For example, he has taught me that things are often not as they appear to be and that there is a relationship between emotional health and being able to choose to give.

Regardless of whether or not we intentionally choose to give or like Kent, choose not to do so, this principle assumes that we always have everything we need within us to live our lives fully and to give to others. In attitudinal healing, acknowledging this is acknowledging the reality of our inner abundance. As Goldsmith says, "At this very moment, we possess all that will unfold as our experience for all the days to come; it is embodied and embraced within our consciousness, and day by day it will unfold and appear as necessary in our human experience. All that God has is ours now."[2]

Giving in the moment, in each instant, occurs naturally when our heart and mind are in alignment. In the moment, one intuits what one is to give. The power of giving comes from the moment, the time of now. Now is the only time there is because now is the time of the heart, the time of intuition, the time of the Divine Source. Goldsmith says that "God has no way of operating except now, as a continuing now."[3] Stephen Levine, expressing this in another way, says:

> Love is the optimum condition for healing. The healer uses whatever he intuits will be of the greatest aid, but his energy cannot come from the mind. His power comes from the openness of his heart. He senses something greater than the body's predicament. He goes to the source out of which all healing occurs, not attempting to disturb or obstruct that

which may allow the next perfect step. He does not
second guess the universe.[4]

Levine writes about giving through speaking silently to someone
from the heart. "Heart-talk" is simply sending loving and accepting
thoughts to a person in need. The purpose of heart-talk is to assure
someone of his okayness. It is not about giving suggestions to the person
or asking him to be or feel any differently than the way he does. A person
is not emotionally and spiritually supported when he is sent worry
thoughts or thoughts that say he is not strong enough to handle the
situation. Thoughts are things and people sense the thoughts that we
have about them. In times of stress and crisis, a person needs supportive
thoughts of love and acceptance, not thoughts that suggest he is weak,
unacceptable or incapable.

The concept of heart-talk relates to this principle because it represents selflessly and intuitively giving in the moment. We can heart-talk
anytime, anywhere, with anyone. What one specifically says reflects
what one feels is intuitively appropriate. Like Levine, I have found this
to be a powerful, nonintrusive and loving way to give. In the course of the
day one can witness several stressful situations, such as a speeding
driver, a mentally ill person living on the street, an overwhelmed checker
in the grocery store. One can heart-talk with them. One can heart-talk at
home or in the work setting. Parents who use heart-talk with their
troubled children and teenagers have found this method particularly
helpful.

Another way to give in the moment is through *kything*. This term
was first used by a cherubim angel, Proginoskes, with Meg, a teenage girl,
in Madeleine L'Engle's novel *The Wind in the Door*.[5] Kything is a way to
communicate with someone spirit-to-spirit. It is a way to be spiritually
present with another person. Psychologists Louis Savary and Patricia
Berne describe kything as "joining freely and lovingly to each other at the
level of spirit. Although kything is a very elementary spiritual act, it is an
affirmation and an experience of a profound union."[6] They recommend
affirming, "I am present to your spirit" when kything. Spiritually joining
with someone can take the form of imaging two people in a bubble of
divine light, placing a person in one's heart, or using any other image
that facilitates being in communion, spirit-to-spirit.

Above all, this principle asks us to trust the now of our life, to see
the beauty of our process, right now as it is – not as it has been, not as it
will be, but as it is right now. By acknowledging that healing resources
are ever present within us, we live our life fully, today. Our process is like

that of the butterfly, which out of a cocoon of darkness, emerges with a fresh and beautiful life. Every step of our transformational process is necessary. In our depths, we have the healing power and the strength for renewed living and for living fully each instant. In this way, we give the highest good to ourselves and to others.

WHAT IS MY ATTITUDE?

Contemplate the following questions and write about your feelings in a journal.

1. How securely do I feel connected with my intuition?

2. How would I describe my own heart-mind alignment?

3. How aware am I of being in the moment? What distracts me from being in the now?

4. Am I aware of giving in my personal life? Work life?

5. What relationship do I see between giving and my emotional and spiritual health?

6. How do I strengthen my connection to the moment?

7. Have I ever experienced selfless action and giving without expectations?

PRACTICING THE PRINCIPLE

Select the exercises that best facilitate and support your healing process, writing your responses in a journal. You may want to prerecord the visualization exercises.

1. The function of contemplative meditation is to strengthen the receptivity to the place of truth that resides within. In silence, place yourself in a state of receptivity, listening and waiting. You may contemplate a thought, a situation, a request, an idea. State your

need simply; close your eyes and sit in stillness. If at first nothing happens and you receive no response, do not be disturbed. Something is happening. It is only a question of when a response will be made known.

Contemplate for one to five minutes on one topic a day and then go about your business. Select the topic from the following suggestions or use one of your own.

Giving	Selfless action
Living life fully	Heart consciousness
Inner strength	Emotional well-being
Healing	Spiritual well-being
Heart-mind alignment	God
Timelessness	Silence
Now	Love

Write in your journal any awarenesses you had about the topic you contemplated during the day. Be aware that some insights may come to you from within or there may be visible responses in the external world. For example, one day I was contemplating self-worth and on my way to work, I passed a car with a sticker that said, "If you knew me you'd love me."

2. With your journal in hand, go for a walk among people or go on an errand. In a very natural and unassuming way, be aware of comments you hear people making. Viewing these conversations as teachings the universe may be giving to you, make a note of the messages. For example, one day while waiting for a stop light to change, I overheard two men talking. One said, "One thing relates to another, it all fits together very logically." And, the other man said, "Yes, it sure does. There's no sense in making learning something so hard when it doesn't have to be." I was reminded in that instant of my tendency to view life as a complicated impossibility and had been thinking so just that day!

3. Think of some way to remind yourself to be in the present moment. This might be writing yourself messages on small cards and placing them in various locations at home or at work. Or, you might set your wrist watch alarm to go off periodically or wear a piece of jewelry, like a noisy bracelet, that attracts your attention occasionally.

4. Sit in silence and picture yourself among those people who play an important role in your personal and work life, either in the past or in the present. See yourself approaching each person and giving him something which symbolizes your love. Give a gift to everyone, including those with whom you are in conflict. Make all the gifts big and wonderful, extraordinarily special, something that will serve each person beyond his dreams. Picture each person accepting your gift. Picture his excitement, gratitude and joy.

5. Select someone (or do this with several people) about whom you are presently concerned or someone with whom you have a conflict in your personal or work life. Close your eyes. Place your consciousness in your heart. Silently speak from your heart and say comforting and reassuring words to this person. Do not ask him to change his behavior, give him any suggestions or offer your point of view. Just reassure him, accept him. Send him love and a sense of okayness. You can do this exercise when you are actually with the person, talking with him by phone or when thinking about him.

6. Ask someone to join you in an experiment of only using the present tense when talking. Only speak about the present using present tense; do not refer to the past or the future. Spend at least a half hour doing this. After the exercise is complete, discuss the experience with one another and ask yourselves the following questions:

  a. How comfortable did I feel only talking about the present?

  b. Did I become more aware of my senses of hearing, vision, taste, smell and touch?

  c. Did I become more aware of my emotions?

  d. Did I forget and return to talking about the past or future?

  e. Did I notice any changes in sentence structure and the content of my speech?

7. To review what it means to be of service to others within the context of attitudinal healing, reread Chapter Four.

HAVE I HEALED MY ATTITUDE?

After practicing the above exercises, contemplate the following questions and write about your feelings in a journal.

1. Am I using contemplation more in my life?

2. Have I become more aware of the present moment when I am with people or alone?

3. Has my eye contact improved when I am with people?

4. Do I experience giving in a more spontaneous way?

5. Am I experiencing more stillness in my meditation?

6. Do I use heart-talk as a way of giving in my personal and work life?

7. Have I experienced any shift in my awareness of living life fully and in the moment?

APPLYING THE PRINCIPLE IN SERVICE

This principle addresses the spirit of giving – the facilitator's motivation for serving others. When you hold the sacred trust of giving in service to others, you live in the spirit of the moment. Your heart and mind are in balance and you are guided from within. You have an inner sense of knowing that the highest good is served for all concerned. You serve with a sense of joy and spontaneity. You know that to extend love is enough.

If you lose sight of the spirit of giving, you are probably experiencing the psychological and spiritual phenomenon known as burnout. Burnout occurs when you find yourself so overburdened with personal responsibility in the helping process that you begin to feel exhausted, frustrated, unnurtured, apathetic and overwhelmed. Your heart begins to close down, you become irritable and impatient, and you lose all joy and inspiration for your work. You begin to have such thoughts as, "Well, what about me? I'm getting nowhere. What I'm doing isn't helping anybody. I don't know what I'll do if anyone asks me to do one more thing. No one appreciates me. I'm tired of having to take care of all these people's needs – why don't they take care of themselves?"

As a facilitator, you can experience burnout for any of the following reasons:

1. You have forgotten to have compassion for yourself by continuing your own inner work.

When you do not continue your own inner work, you fail to recognize your limits and to acknowledge your own physical, emotional and spiritual needs. You forget to forgive yourself for the fearful, doubtful and judgemental thoughts you have had about yourself and the people you serve. You will maintain your energy, your inspiration and your joy by continually revitalizing your own physical, emotional and spiritual selves through your practice of emotional and spiritual disciplines. The compassion you have for others is a direct reflection of the compassion you have for yourself. Relieving the suffering of others begins with attending to the relief of your own.

2. You have forgotten to be in your Witness Self.

Whenever you identify with the problem of the person you are facilitating, you begin to react instead of respond. You become focused on your own unmet needs. An inner conflict occurs because you cannot attend to your own emotional or spiritual needs at the same time you are attending to those of the person you are facilitating. You will experience psychological stress when your attention is divided and you are not focused and present in the moment. You will sense that the person you are facilitating knows you are not fully listening or fully present. You will then judge yourself for this failure and this judgement becomes a further stress. You have forgotten to simply observe the person's process, to remain quiet and open.

3. You have lost sight of the inner strength of the person you are helping.

The goal of facilitating is to support the person in being his own best therapist. This goal assumes that the person being facilitated has all the inner resources he needs to successfully work through his process. When you forget to honor the healing process of the other person, you will see him as weak and incapable. You will then begin to feel totally responsible for the person's healing and well-being. This struggle of responsibility creates emotional fatigue and can overwhelm you. You may succumb to your ego needs to be powerful, needed, worthy and responsible, and you may see yourself as the rescuer, the savior and the healer.

4. You have expectations of outcome.

When your motivation is to change a person's consciousness in a certain way, you will be met with resistance. A facilitator who has expectations of results attempts to meet the resistance of the person by attempting to resist the resistance. When you insist on pushing through the resistance, on imposing your will, your desires and wishes, you will soon become exhausted, physically and emotionally. You will also have created a separation of purpose between yourself and the person you are facilitating because you will want confirmation of your expectations and will want your results satisfied, measured and applauded. This separation creates a conflict and leads to further stress. You have forgotten that the results are unknowable. You have forgotten to be focused on the process and not the product. You have simply forgotten to let the expectations that come to your mind pass by.

5. You have forgotten the joy and spontaneity of being of service.

When you take the supportive process very, very seriously and begin to anticipate the future outcome and rewards of your work, you will lose sight of the present moment. In doing so, you will not experience the lightness, the joy and the spontaneity that can occur when facilitating someone. Being in the Witness Self gives a sense of freedom as you observe the ebb and flow of the supportive process. To simply see the absurd side of life events and of your own reactions can bring the healing gift of humor and laughter into the supportive relationship.

6. You have forgotten your primary motivation for being of service.

When you have as your motivation and reason for helping others the fulfillment of your own needs or expectations of outcome, you will become frustrated and discouraged. When you shift your perspective and call on a deeper, more universal and less personal motivation, you will experience a sense of inner peace and trust. You will recognize that you had temporarily forgotten that your reason for facilitating is to love others. Extending love is enough.

7. You think that you are the doer.

When you identify yourself as the doer, the source of the service, you feel personally responsible for the other person. You believe that success and failure are determined by your efforts alone – you did it, you were the source of what happened. Because maintaining this attitude requires much energy, you will soon become physically and emotionally fatigued. Shifting to the place of the Witness Self, you can recognize that you are not the doer, that the Divine Source flowing through you and the person you are supporting is the doer. Therefore, it is not your responsibility but that of the Divine Source. You need to remind yourself not to take on the unnecessary burden of being the doer. If you forget and attempt to be the doer, you must then be compassionate with yourself.

HOW AM I DOING?

Periodically assess your progress in applying this principle in service to others. Note your concerns, questions and feelings in a journal.

1. Am I actively continuing my own inner work and do I see how it relates to supporting someone?

2. Am I aware of signs of burnout within myself and do I respond to these signs responsibly?

3. Am I increasingly aware of being in the Witness Self when I am supporting someone?

4. Do I increasingly view the person I am supporting as having inner strength and resources?

5. Am I aware of choosing what it is I want to give in the supportive relationship?

6. Am I increasingly aware of giving from a selfless, intuitive place in the supportive relationship?

7. Do I experience having fewer expectations of outcome when I am with a person and less need to measure my work? Is it okay with me not to know what the results might be?

8. Do I keep my motivation for being of service in focus?

9. Am I increasingly aware of the times I slip into thinking I am the doer?

10. Do I find myself using heart-talk when I support someone?

Chapter Ten

*T he greatest revolution of our generation
is the discovery that human beings, by
changing the inner attitudes of their
minds, can change the outer aspects of
their lives.*

William James

WE CAN LEARN TO LOVE OURSELVES AND OTHERS BY FORGIVING RATHER THAN JUDGING

BASIC TENETS

1. *Forgiveness is being able to hold ourselves and others in our heart regardless of what has happened.*

2. *It is natural to want to forgive and to be forgiven.*

3. *Forgiveness is the willingness to perceive ourselves and others as either expressing love or giving a call for love.*

4. *Forgiveness does not deny what has happened. It is the willingness to search for a truth that lies beyond the situation.*

5. *Forgiveness reduces stress and positively affects the physical health of an individual.*

6. *Forgiveness is seeing the painful actions of ourselves and others as*

coming from unhealed emotional wounds, usually stemming from childhood.

7. *Forgiveness is a state of being, an attitude, and does not imply a specific action to be taken on the part of the one forgiving or the one being forgiven.*

8. *Judgement is defined as any belief, thought, evaluation or condemnation that results in separation and isolation from ourselves or one another.*

9. *Forgiveness is grace and therefore is not something you "do" but something that reveals itself.*

10. *The first step in releasing judgemental thoughts involves both acknowledging and observing them.*

THE PRINCIPLE'S MESSAGE

When Janet sat across from me in a workshop I was leading and began her process, I was impressed with how calmly and confidently she stated her need to do grief work relating to the death of her sixteen-year-old daughter. I did not know that what was about to unfold was the most profound example of forgiveness that I had ever heard.

Eighteen years ago Janet's daughter, Marcie, had been brutally murdered; her body was found floating in a river. The murderer was identified as a man in Marcie's hometown. The family was enraged and expressed their rage through verbal attacks and multi-million dollar law suits against the assailant and the legal system. In a fit of rage and grief, Janet's husband almost killed the murderer. For fourteen years, the members of the family drained all of their energy by hating this man. They wanted revenge for the horror he had brought into their lives. Their grief and rage were all consuming.

Finally, Janet and her husband decided to visit the murderer in prison and to confront him. They wanted to know why he had committed the crime and why Marcie was the victim.

What took place in that encounter was something very unexpected. As Janet and her husband faced this man, the hatred between them suddenly fell away and they felt love and care for him. In an instant, they saw his humanness, his pain and his grief. They felt not hatred and revenge but great compassion and love. The three of them hugged and sobbed out of pain for the tragedy that they shared. They decided to periodically visit him and in the course of time the three of them have talked openly about what happened and why.

By the time that Janet came to my workshop she was ready to complete another part of her grieving process by focusing on the healing needed within the family unit. Janet said she had come to see that she had been extremely successful in teaching her children to hate and that as a result they have continued to suffer. Janet has made a commitment to create the healing of this hatred within the family. She has decided to be an example of unconditional love in order to reverse her prior teaching.

Janet is now a counselor at a homicide crisis center where she assists families of murdered children. From Janet's point of view, there is not a murderer in prison who does not want to confront the family he harmed and to be forgiven by them. In order to forgive the murderer, family members have to reconsider their beliefs about the assailant and be willing to see him differently.

Janet's story teaches us the true meaning of forgiveness. Forgiveness occurred because the people involved, the "victims," opened their hearts to the person they felt had hurt them. They saw the person through their hearts as someone who in his own right was worthy of compassion, healing and love. Janet clearly saw that the murderer was no different than herself, a person searching for love and value in his life.

Dostoyevsky, upon being released from the Siberian prison where he lived and worked with Russia's worst criminals, said:

> Prison saved me....It was a good school....I became a completely new person. . . .I have no complaint at all. It strengthened my faith and awakened my love for those who bear all their suffering with patience. . . .
>
> The prisoners prayed devoutly, and every time they brought with them a poor kopeck to buy candles or to make an offering. "I too am a man," the convict may have thought as he threw his small coin into the collection box, "in God's eyes we are all equal." After morning Mass, we took Communion. When the priest, wafer in hand, spoke the words, "Receive me Lord, even as a thief," nearly everyone kneeled immediately and the chains clanked, for each man understood the words to be directed specifically at him.[1]

Dostoyevsky saw the greatness even in the most terrible criminal. Throughout his novels, a part of him seems to identify with the criminal.

Uli Derickson, the TWA flight attendant who risked her life in 1985 to keep hijackers from killing more people on Flight 847 as it crisscrossed the Mediterranean for 55 hours said, "I always thought of these men as human beings. As brutal as they were (the hijackers killed a Navy diver, beat two other passengers and terrorized everybody), I never let myself think of them as animals. I always tried to appeal to their hearts."[2]

We add greatly to our mental and emotional suffering when we do not forgive. Ruth Carter Stapleton, a well-known minister and healer in the sixties and seventies, wrote that "if we refuse to forgive, we the offended will lose more than the offender." She explains:

> Whatever we cannot forgive we are doomed one day to live. The person who refuses to forgive the gossip eventually becomes a gossip. The one who cannot forgive a betrayal becomes a betrayer. The reason for this is that the inability to forgive a frailty in another person indicates that we have the same negative condition existing in us. If we had forgiven that weakness in another, the act of forgiveness would have acted as an antidote to our own weakness.[3]

The attitude of true forgiveness does not mean that we deny what has happened. Denial is always unhealthy and leads only to the festering of the wounds. Forgiveness does not imply that criminals be allowed to go free or that someone who has harmed us psychologically or physically be allowed to continue to do so. That is just as damaging psychologically and spiritually to the other person as it is to ourselves.

Forgiveness does not assume a certain action is taken. The story of Julia and David in Chapter Seven exemplifies forgiveness as a process, not an action. Forgiveness is a gift we give ourselves. When David forgave Julia for being Asian, he forgave himself for his own hatred and anger which he had been hiding under the label "Asian." The gift of forgiveness freed him from this burden and in this process freed Julia also.

Forgiveness is a process of opening our hearts and having compassion that results in the mind letting go of grievances. When we have compassion for another person, we have compassion for ourselves. It is always painful to hold another person out of our heart. It is painful to be held out of somebody's heart. It is painful to hold oneself out of one's heart.

Most of all, forgiveness is grace in action. Grace does not come from without, from above, from elsewhere. Grace comes from within us. When we welcome grace into our lives, grievances fall away, the veil lifts, the heart opens. The heart and mind come into alignment so feelings and thoughts match. Grace is the energy of forgiveness, an energy that melts away grievances and pain and opens the space for another way to view the event. Grace is the source of the experience of forgiveness.

WHAT IS MY ATTITUDE?

Contemplate the following questions and write about your feelings in a journal.

1. Have I had the experience of forgiveness as defined in the previous section?

2. Do I see myself as a person who has a great deal of forgiving to do?

3. Have I had the experience of having my heart open to others, particularly those towards whom I hold a grievance?

4. What do I feel I need to forgive myself for?

5. What progress have I seen in my forgiveness process the past five years?

6. What do I see as the next step in my forgiveness process?

7. How conscious am I of the presence of grace in my life?

PRACTICING THE PRINCIPLE

Select the exercises that best facilitate and support your healing process, writing your responses in a journal. You may want to prerecord the visualization exercises.

1. For three consecutive nights, do the following: Light a white candle in a darkened room. Look at the candle with your eyes slightly open so you see some of the candle's glowing light. In your mind, address the person toward whom you feel conflict, stating briefly your feelings to him, such as, "Dad, I know things have not gone well between the two of us. I feel so hurt when I think of you and I know I have not been honest with you." Then, for half an hour, say the following over and over, "Dad, I wish you the best possible evolution. Dad, I wish you the best possible evolution." (This exercise is believed to be from a Buddhist tradition).

2. Stephen Levine suggests the following exercise in *Who Dies?*:

> Imagine that you are lying in an emergency room, critically injured, unable to speak or move, the concerned faces of your loved ones floating above you, the pain beginning to dull from the morphine just injected. You wish to reach out to tell them something, to finish your business, to say good-bye, to cut through years of partial communication.
>
> What would you say? Think of what has remained unsaid and share that each day with those you love. Don't hesitate.[4]

3. Create a clear picture in your mind of the person toward whom you feel resentment. See yourself interact with that person.

Picture good things happening to that person. See him receiving love and attention and gifts from others.

Be aware of your own reactions. If you have difficulty seeing good things happening to the person, it is a natural reaction. It will become easier with practice.

Think about the role you have played in this stressful relationship and how you might reinterpret the person's behavior. Imagine how the situation might look from the other person's point of view.

Tell yourself you will carry this new understanding with you.

4. Just before falling asleep, go through the events of the day from night back to morning. Acknowledge any feelings that arise about these events. Then ask yourself to have a healing dream regarding a relationship in which you feel conflict. Say three times, "I request a healing dream about _____." Then say three times, "I will remember my dreams." Record your dreams and spend some time working with them.

The dream(s) may give you a solution, may redefine the problem/ issue, may represent alternatives, may give you a deeper understanding or may give you a soothing, healing feeling that seems to replace the feelings of conflict. Some people just wake up feeling better but have no specific recall of any dreams. In general, welcoming healing into your life always has a constructive, positive effect – and much of this can be done at night. While asleep, our bodies and our emotions can and do heal.

The following are some facilitating questions that may assist you in working with your dream(s):

a. When you reexperience the feelings you had in the dream, what do they remind you of in your current life? What would you guess the dream is about?

b. What literal meaning might the dream have?

c. Would you describe the first scene of the dream? This is often a statement or description of the problem/issue/situation/ obstacle you are having or facing in your life, i.e., something that is giving you trouble. The first scene of the dream tells you what the dream is going to be about – the topic being addressed.

What are the middle scenes? These are aspects of the problem, the development of the plot, so to speak. Middle scenes can define and describe various aspects of the problem.

What is the final scene of the dream? This represents or describes the solution, resolution or way to overcome the problem or obstacle described in the first scene. It is helpful sometimes to work with the first and last scenes first, and then the middle ones to gain some direction on what the dream is about.

d. Who is _____? What do you associate with each person in the dream? Describe them from your perspective. Take nothing for granted so as to discover crucial associations to the major characters.

What is the person like? If the dream figure is unknown to you, ask what kind of person you would imagine the person to be.

Can you recognize or feel that part of you which is like this person? Most dream figures represent an aspect of the dreamer, so this person represents an aspect of yourself.

What is your relationship with this person like?

Can you speak as if you were this person in the dream by becoming that person?

e. Can you define each major object in the dream? Again, speak as if you were this object in the dream.

f. Can you give the dream a title as if it were a play or novel to assist you in gleaning the essence of the dream's message?

5. On a sheet of paper, list all the things you forgive yourself for, writing "I forgive myself for_____, I forgive myself for_____, I forgive myself for_____." List not only general feelings and attitudes but also specific events about which you have regret. Set the paper aside. Look at the list again the next day. Add more things that have come to your mind. Be honest and complete. Set the paper aside. Look at it again on the third day and add further items if necessary. Burn or destroy the list on the third day with an attitude of compassion for yourself and all those involved on the list. Affirm that you release yourself from all pain of unforgiveness and that everything is all right.

You can also do this exercise with a trusted friend, expressing what you feel you need to forgive yourself for until you have a sense of completion. Your trusted friend responds "You are forgiven" after each item you share. Ask your friend to encourage you to be specific should your responses become general. For example, a general statement would be "I forgive myself for hitting Tommy"; the specific would be ". . . for hitting Tommy when he spilled his milk."

6. Imagine yourself floating and moving among gray clouds, with the clouds representing the various grievances you hold against yourself and others. See yourself glide through the clouds, bumping into them ever so gently. You notice the clouds do not harm you; they brush against your cheeks, against your face. You gently push them aside as you move through them. As time passes you begin to see that there is a light beyond the clouds and you begin moving towards the light. As the gray clouds continue to bump into you, you continue to let them bounce off and move aside ever so gently. Finally, you begin to see the full brilliance of the light and you move into it, knowing you are safe, that you are in the light.

HAVE I HEALED MY ATTITUDE?

After practicing the above exercises, contemplate the following questions and write about your feelings in a journal.

1. Am I more aware of when I exclude someone from my heart?

2. Do I feel any softening of my heart towards those whom I have grievances?

3. Do I have more compassion and patience for myself?

4. Am I better able to just watch my judging thoughts as they pass through my mind as opposed to dwelling on them?

5. Are people saying to me that I seem more at peace with myself?

6. Am I less aware of viewing the world as made up of victims and victimizers?

7. Am I better able to choose a loving thought as opposed to a judgemental one?

APPLYING THE PRINCIPLE IN SERVICE

Practicing forgiveness always necessitates suspending judgement of oneself and others. By vigilant monitoring of one's thoughts, it is possible to listen to and support someone without evaluating or judging. In this way, you make room to hold the person in your heart and in the thought of forgiveness.

I once visited the classroom of an elementary school teacher because I had been told that she applied the attitudinal healing principles. When I walked into the room, I noticed a large sign hanging from the middle of the ceiling. Large letters spelled out JUDGEMENT. Curious, I asked her about it. "Oh yes," she replied, "we suspend judgement in second grade."

Most of us were not so fortunate as to be taught nonjudgemental attitudes so young. Long years of practice make it tempting to continue to critique, categorize and compare ourselves and others. This is especially tempting when someone asks for help. Engaging in judgemental thoughts or advice does not create a safe place for the person to share his experiences or to safely explore alternatives, understanding, insights and options. As a facilitator, you may be perpetually forgiving yourself for these judgements. The goal is to cultivate the witness part of the mind that watches these thoughts and gently lets them pass by. In this way, the mind tends to become more silent and the intuitive hunches as to what to do or say emerge more clearly.

You also can invite grace into the supportive relationship and invite the person to do so as well. This invitation to grace is a direct invitation to the Divine Source. When you love yourself enough to open your heart to the possibility of forgiveness, you open the way for that Source to heal. This assistance speeds and eases the healing process. Grace comes totally unmerited by anything you have done; it is your love essence at work and is available the moment you truly open to its possibility.

Only to the extent that you have experienced forgiveness personally will you be able to provide a large enough space for the person you are working with to do so as well. If you, for example, have forgiven yourself for addictions to food, substances or relationships, you will become a natural vehicle for the same kind of healing in others. This is why recovering alcoholics can be so effective with practicing alcoholics. If you have healed your relationship with your father, for example, you know that it is possible and therefore hold the space of possibility for the person you work with.

In my own life I have been emotionally healed of severe psychological and spiritual abuse and neglect. Therefore, I hold the space and the possibility for emotional and spiritual healing for anyone who has a similar personal history. Knowing that healing is possible, that it is a reality, I naturally carry that thought or that energy with me.

As a facilitator, you need to contemplate your own life experiences, making mental note of those particular human conditions for which you are an avenue of healing. You might find it helpful to list these conditions, such as, "I know what it is like to be betrayed. I know what it is like to grow up without a father. I know what it is like to be an alcoholic. I know what it is like to move thirteen times in fifteen years. I know what it is like to experience the joy of forgiveness of a grievance I thought was impossible to forgive." This list reflects the multitude of human conditions for which you can cultivate compassion, not only for yourself, but for others. This list also shows you the magnitude of the gifts that have come out of your own pain and suffering which you now have to offer others.

HOW AM I DOING?

Periodically assess your progress in applying this principle in service to others. Note your concerns, questions and feelings in a journal.

1. Was I conscious of keeping my heart open during the time I was with the person I was supporting?

2. Was I able to really hear the person's experience, suspending judgement and opening to hear from within what I was to say or do?

3. Was I able to observe the similarity of the person's experiences to mine yet not need to interrupt by sharing my own story?

4. Have I become more forgiving of myself as a result of hearing the experiences of another person?

5. Have I been strengthening the use of my Witness Self through regular meditation?

6. Have I invited and welcomed grace into the supportive relationship and do I experience this as a reality?

7. Am I better able to see the truth behind a situation rather than becoming focused on the events themselves?

Chapter Eleven

$\mathcal{A}$ nother opportunity was given you – as a favour and as a burden. The question is not: why did it happen this way, or where is it going to lead you, or what is the price you will have to pay. It is simply: _how_ are you making use of it. And about that there is only _one_ who can judge.

Dag Hammarskjöld

Principle Seven

WE CAN BECOME LOVE-FINDERS RATHER THAN FAULT-FINDERS

BASIC TENETS

1. *To love-find is to see beyond the personality to the love essence of ourselves and others.*

2. *To fault-find is to see the personality only.*

3. *To love-find is to see the value and learning opportunity in every circumstance.*

4. *To fault-find is to see oneself and others as a victim of circumstance.*

5. *Both love-finding and fault-finding can crystallize into habit and therefore become a way of life.*

6. *One can choose to feed the thoughts of love-finding or of fault-finding.*

7. *Every genuine loving thought about ourselves or others is saved in the universe.*

8. *The faults that we see in others mirror the faults we see in ourselves. This is the law of projection.*

157

9. *The love we see in others mirrors the love we know is within ourselves. This is the law of extension.*

10. *Acknowledging love-finds strengthens and nurtures one's emotional and spiritual well-being.*

THE PRINCIPLE'S MESSAGE

I have always thought of this principle as the valentine principle because of an event that occurred several years ago.

Following a lecture I gave, Ned, a well-educated retired gentleman, called and asked me to see Mary, his wife of forty-one years. He described Mary as being very troubled and suggested the possibility that she might be mentally ill. The picture he painted of Mary's mental condition was so bleak that I agreed to see her immediately. To my surprise instead of the person he had described I saw a beautiful soul and loving spirit who was also very unhappy in her marriage.

After my initial meeting with Mary, I told Ned that I would only continue seeing her if he also came. Initially he was not at all pleased with my stipulation and saw no need for his involvement but he agreed in order to be a "good sport."

During the first sessions Mary and Ned exchanged barrages of faults. All the wrong-doings of forty-one years were thrown by each at the other. In order to make peaceful arbitration possible, I established a list of communication ground rules. In the following weeks as they each faithfully practiced these guidelines, their conflicts began to be resolved. Before my eyes, they fell in love again!

Mary was particularly fond of the guideline about being a love-finder rather than a fault-finder. She felt a great commitment to applying this in her daily life. Later when she was a participant in the Institute's facilitator training course, it was this principle she chose to present to the group as part of her training. Mary presented her lesson on love-finding on February 7. Three days later she died suddenly of a heart attack. On Valentine's Day her life was honored in a memorial service.

In talking together, Ned and I both realized that during the six months the three of us had worked together, Mary had been focusing on "finishing business" in her life by healing her relationship with Ned and with other family members. The family saw her as having been happier than she ever had been. Mary and Ned spent the last six months of her life learning to be and being love-finders. The lesson and its practice brought Mary and Ned peace and healing, which they also had shared with those around them.

Our minds are strongly programmed to find fault. Most of us have been exposed to years of being programmed to have thoughts that compare, evaluate, condemn and categorize. We become master fault-finders. We find fault with the weather, news, family members, repair-men, clothes and bodies. How often are our thoughts and words acknowledgements or appreciations to another person or to ourselves?

Even when the mind hears something positive, it will want to counteract with finding a fault. One day when I was patiently waiting at a bus stop, a forlorn looking elderly woman sat down next to me. As I had been wanting to become more of a love-finder, I decided to start a friendly conversation with her. I said, "Umm, do you think it will rain today?" Without skipping a beat, she replied, "Humph! How do I know? I ain't no prophet."

An amusing story in Roy Pinyoun's book *Greener Pastures* clearly demonstrates how strong our tendency to fault-find can be.

A barber was giving a man a haircut and the barber said, "Are you taking a vacation this year?" The man in the chair said, "Yes, in fact my wife and I are flying to Rome tomorrow for a couple of weeks." Barber: "How are you going?" Customer: "By United." Barber: "Don't go by United. The service is poor, the food is lousy, the stewardesses are ugly and it'll be rough all the way. Where are you staying in Rome?" Customer: "At the Hilton." Barber: "Don't stay there – you won't like it. The food is no good, the beds are hard and nobody will pay atten-tion to you. You can find a better place to stay than that. What are you going to do in Rome?" Cus-tomer: "We thought we would try to get an audi-ence with the Pope." Barber: "Take my advice, don't waste your time; you'll never get near him. There'll be ten thousand Italians milling around smelling like garlic. You'll wish you had never gone near the place." The customer paid his bill and walked out.

Three weeks later, he was back. Barber: "Did you go to Italy?" Customer: "Yep." Barber: "How did you

go to Italy?" Customer: "We went by United. It was
a wonderful trip, smooth sailing all the way. The
food was excellent, the service great and the stewardesses were outstanding. Couldn't have been
better." Barber: "Where did you stay?" Customer:
"At the Hilton. It's a beautiful place, the food was
terrific, the beds were soft and the accommodations
were wonderful!" Barber: "Did you see the Pope?"
Customer: "Yes, we did. We had a good half hour
with him. There were only about a half dozen
people and we didn't have to wait more than five
minutes. It was the highlight of the trip." Barber:
"Well, what did he say?" Customer: "As I knelt at
his feet to receive his blessing, he looked at me and
said, "For Pete's sake, man! Where did you get that
miserable haircut?"[1]

Fault-finding is rarely more prevalent than it is within families.
Relatives are criticized, behavior is judged, and evaluations and compari-
sons are made. Early in our life this critical attitude and way of communicating becomes a habit of the mind. There is a tendency to believe that
saying something positive about another family member will inflate the
person's ego or that good thoughts are assumed and do not have to be
acknowledged. This is very damaging to the human psyche. The psyche
needs to be nurtured and loved, by others and by ourselves. The psyche
is strengthened when we acknowledge its value and validate its purpose.

There is no way we can perceive faults in others if we have not first
seen that fault within ourselves. Because we hold ourselves guilty for
having that fault we readily see it in others. This is the law of projection.
Understanding this law allows us to use it advantageously in our own
learning. Each time we find fault or make a judgement about another
person, we need to acknowledge that same fault in ourself. We can view
the fault as providing another lesson to learn, another fear or grievance
to be released.

I love plants. At one time I had about forty of them beautifully
arranged in the corner of my office at the university. One day a woman
came to see me and upon looking at the display of green, healthy plants,
she pointed to one of them and said, "Susan, that plant needs watering."
Inside, I felt great anger towards her for finding fault with one of my
plants. Later when I reflected on the incident and examined my upset, I
gained two insights about my reaction, both of which represented old

grievances and fault-finding against myself and others. The first was that I heard her remark as saying that I was thoughtless. The plants represented living things to me that need care and nurturing. By my intense emotional reaction to her comment, I realized I was holding grievances against myself for all the times in my life I had been thoughtless towards living things and towards all those people I felt had been thoughtless towards me. I also projected onto her remark that she was correcting me for a wrong I had done. At the time, I was very sensitive to being corrected. I saw I was still holding a grievance against my own "corrector self" and against people in my childhood whom I felt were always correcting me. My healing work involved forgiving myself and others for what I perceived had been done to me. This entire process was a result of recognizing my projections onto this woman's remark.

To understand the law of projection and to use its messages positively in our growth, we look beyond the form of a situation to the message it carries. We must abstract out the theme of the event and then ask ourselves what faults or grievances we are finding within ourselves or against others that this event is serving to remind us of. When working with this concept, a man said, "Do you mean that if I react in great anger to hearing about a person raping someone, that I am a rapist, too?" "Perhaps not in the literal sense," he was told, "but rape is symbolic of imposing one's will onto people and intruding on their space. Have you ever done that?"

We can project our faults or grievances onto organizations, events, objects, ideas and bodies, as well as individuals. If for example, we react with great negativity to how an organization is run and question its integrity, we may find it helpful to ask ourselves how we feel about our own organizational skills and the integrity with which we live our public or business life.

WHAT IS MY ATTITUDE?

Contemplate the following questions and write about your feelings in a journal.

1. How do I define a love-finder?

2. How do I define a fault-finder?

3. What are some of the reasons I find fault with myself and others?

4. In what situations do I fault-find?

5. Do I see myself as more of a fault-finder or love-finder?

6. What are some of the ways I express love-finds to myself and to others?

7. Am I aware of my projections onto people, places and things? What are some of these projections?

PRACTICING THE PRINCIPLE

Select the exercises that best facilitate and support your healing process, writing your responses in a journal. You may want to prerecord the visualization exercises.

1. Select a situation in which you were aware of being a fault-finder. Write the situation down and then close your eyes and relive the events, focusing on what was said and done and what your feelings and thoughts were at the time. Then write down what seemed most important to you about this situation.

Close your eyes again, reliving the situation but this time focus on finding at least one love-find. The love-find may be very subtle but stay with the event until one comes to you.

Now write down the love-find that seemed most important for you to be aware of in that situation.

2. At the end of each day for a week, acknowledge any growth you have noticed about yourself by writing it down in list form. This needs to be a genuine acknowledgement about yourself and may be very subtle, even if it is something like "I acknowledge myself for getting up when the alarm went off the first time" or "I acknowledge myself for making an appointment to have my taxes done" or "I acknowledge myself for meditating ten minutes today."

3. Select a person with whom you would like to have a more harmonious relationship. In one column write the faults you find about that person. In an adjacent column, write some love-finds.

Note which is the longer list. If the list of fault-finds is longer than the list of love-finds, continue with the process until both lists are of the same length. Periodically refer back to the list and see if you can add further love-finds.

4. Draw a large rectangle on a sheet of paper to represent a blackboard. Select a person you find fault with and list those faults on the board. Crumple the paper and either throw it away or burn it. Then draw another large rectangle to once again represent a blackboard. This time open your heart to sense what it is the person would like you to know or understand about him that would help you understand his behavior. Write these thoughts on the board. Note your willingness to do this. You may have to return to this paper periodically and add additional thoughts.

5. Write five love-find affirmations about yourself on a small card and carry these with you for a week. In times of stress or when you find yourself fault-finding, reread the card. When you write your affirmations, use short positive statements in present tense, such as "I am seeing myself as valuable and worthy."

6. Light a candle at the end of the day for the health and well-being of any person you fault-finded during the day, honoring the highest good of that person. You might want to affirm, "I honor (name) and his value in the world." Then allow yourself to stop thinking about the person and what injustice you might have felt. Let the prayer and affirmation do the healing work.

HAVE I HEALED MY ATTITUDE?

After practicing the above exercises, contemplate the following questions and write about your feelings in a journal.

1. Am I more aware of my fault-finding thoughts and the amount of time and the situations in which I engage in them?

2. Am I more aware of the many forms of love-finds and what the forms are that I find myself using?

3. Am I able to recognize my projections and constructively use them for my own growth?

4. Do I have more of an inner sense of self-acceptance and do I find myself accepting others more?

5. What shifts have I observed in those relationships in which I have been acknowledging love-finds?

6. Have others affirmed my love-find attitude by acknowledging me more?

7. Am I willing to take time every day to acknowledge my own growth and accomplishments?

APPLYING THE PRINCIPLE IN SERVICE

Our Institute incorporates the communication guidelines which emerged from my work with Mary and Ned into all of our individual and group work. We have found them to be extremely helpful in strengthening and healing our own personal and work relationships as well as our relationships with those whom we support. Often we share these guidelines with the persons we are supporting as they, too, may find them useful in their personal and work life relationships.

COMMUNICATION GUIDELINES

1. Share from your own experience, speaking from the "Responsible I."

2. Check out assumptions and understandings of the other's point of view.

3. Be alert to use of stopper words and phrases, e.g., you always, you never, every, none, absolutely, every time, no one.

4. Prevent miscommunications with others by making agreements regarding who has what responsibilities in a given situation.

5. Notice use of judgements, justifications, corrections, parent-child communications, defenses, put-downs and attacks.

6. Be an observer of your communications by using your Witness Self.

7. As a listener, check and observe your inner thoughts. Are you really listening? Are you in the present moment? Are you rehearsing what you are going to say and not listening? Are you aware of and honoring the person's timing and pacing?

8. Notice interruptions. Check if the person has completed his expression, verbally and emotionally.

9. Look directly at the person while talking or listening. Be alert to your own and the other's nonverbal messages.

10. Observe your own willingness to learn a new way to communicate, to welcome change and growth, to break old patterns.

11. Appraise honestly the quality and kind of commitment you want in your relationship with another. Observe how you express this commitment in your communications.

12. Ask yourself the following questions in all circumstances, personal and interpersonal:

    • Do I wish to choose my attitude in this situation?

    • Do I choose to be a love-finder or a fault-finder?

    • Is this interaction (verbal or nonverbal) loving to both the other person and myself?

When you are supporting someone, all nature of fault-finding and evaluative thoughts are apt to constantly pass through your mind – "I'm bored . . . I really need to go to the store . . . gosh, that person needs a haircut . . . I really understand what you are saying . . . I really should lose some weight. . . you have many strengths . . . yeah, that happened to me once and my story is quite a bit more interesting than yours . . . I can see you really want to heal your attitude." You choose which thoughts you feed and which ones you don't. To make this choice, you need to become aware of that part of the mind that watches or witnesses your thoughts. In this way you select thoughts that are love-finders or fault-finders.

As a facilitator, you are responsible for your projections in the supportive relationship and for examining how they relate to your own healing process. You need to look at the context in which the upset occurred and upon noting what feelings and thoughts were triggered, search for the grievance or fault you are holding against yourself or another person. Your skill in working with your own projections relates directly to your ability to assist others in looking at theirs. You will need to practice gaining facility in viewing upsets in this way, unless you already are accustomed to looking at life from this perspective.

HOW AM I DOING?

Periodically assess your progress in applying this principle in service to others. Note your concerns, questions and feelings in a journal.

1. Am I fully present for the person I am supporting or is my mind filled with distracting thoughts?

2. How much do I think the other person feels heard?

3. Am I increasingly able to engage my Witness Self?

4. Am I increasingly aware of choosing my thoughts when with a person?

5. Am I able to have love-finding thoughts about myself as a facilitator?

6. Have I increased how much and how often I extend love-finders to others? To myself?

7. Can I more readily recognize my projections and identify what they represent within myself?

8. Do I see the relationship between this principle and the facilitator guideline that says "to extend love is enough"?

Chapter Twelve

E ach tree and leaf and star show how
The universe is part of this one cry,
That every life is noted and is cherished,
And nothing loved is ever lost or perished.

Madeleine L'Engle

WE CAN CHOOSE AND DIRECT OURSELVES TO BE PEACEFUL INSIDE REGARDLESS OF WHAT IS HAPPENING OUTSIDE

BASIC TENETS

1. *To have peace of mind is our primary goal while on earth.*

2. *From the peace in our minds, we extend peace into the world.*

3. *Peace of mind is a result of healing emotional wounds through giving up all thoughts of separation.*

4. *To have peace of mind is to be connected to the Divine Source; this connection is our true identity.*

5. *To give peace, we must be peace; to keep peace, we must give peace away.*

6. *Our safety in this world cannot be found outside of us in the external world; to be safe in this world, we must find safety within our minds. We are safe within our minds when we have inner peace.*

7. *Inner peace has no opposite and is experienced as a quiet mind.*

8. *Inner peace comes from knowing we have the power to choose our attitude in any circumstance. We bring peace to any situation when we bring a peaceful mind.*

9. *Inner peace is knowing we are not our bodies and that our safety does not lie in the physical world.*

10. *Health, in the context of attitudinal healing, is inner peace.*

THE PRINCIPLE'S MESSAGE

This principle is one of the most challenging ones to practice in today's world. From the media and from our own experience living in the world, we sense an absence of physical and emotional safety. Our external world seems filled with danger, whether it be from careless drivers, murderers, swindlers, drug dealers, child abusers, obscene phone callers or enraged customers.

People who work with the public are aware of the unpredictable behavior of humanity. One can feel fooled at every turn, discovering that people and things are not as they appear. We are on constant alert. Fear can literally consume us as we live in this seemingly unsafe world. In addition, we bring into this daily world all our childhood fears, our fears learned in the past.

Fortunately, there is another way to look at the world and at the fear it engenders. This way is not to look for safety in the external world but to look for it within oneself.

My own fears of the outside world were heightened one summer evening fifteen years ago when someone indiscriminately shot through my living room window. The bullet narrowly missed me as I sat on the living room couch. This incident unearthed the tremendous and lifelong fear I had about being physically and psychologically harmed by other people and by external events. Suddenly I was in touch with years of pent-up fears, from childhood through my youth and into my adult years. A friend of mine once told me he thought I was the most fearful person he had ever met. I denied his observation at the time but this shooting incident validated his observation. I was suddenly faced with grappling with an issue I'm sure confronts most of us who live on this earth – fear.

When I examined my fears of the outside world, I observed how desperately I was seeking safety in the world. I wanted people to be safe, machines to be safe, the environment to be safe. The outside world, however, was unpredictable and unreliable. I didn't know when it would next "attack" me. I felt continuously buffeted by the world, not knowing how it was going to treat me. I felt helpless. I did not know any way to live in the world except through fear.

I had been studying dream psychology at the time of the shooting incident and had learned a simple and powerful tool called dream incubation. In dream incubation, you, the dreamer, program your dreams to solve personal problems or to give guidance about issues or decisions. You first write about the issue, viewing it from various perspectives. You empty out your feelings, your logic, your perplexities. Then you write your question in a simple and direct way. My question, at the conclusion of my writing was: "How can I feel safe in a fearful world?"

This is the dream I had that night:

> I am standing next to Jesus. I stand so close to him that we are gently touching, side by side, shoulder to shoulder. We are standing in the middle of a bubble. The bubble feels solid and has a gelatin-like texture. I can see through it very clearly. Suddenly, I notice several very grotesque monster-like animals charging the bubble. I become fearful that they will reach us and harm us. As each monster hits the bubble, however, it dissolves into nothing. Some monsters barely touch the bubble and dissolve, others enter it part way and dissolve, some almost reach us before they dissolve. Monster after monster tries to go through the bubble to reach us and each one dissolves. One monster dissolves only when he is inches away from the two of us.
>
> Jesus then says to me, "As long as you stand beside me, you have nothing to fear."

I awoke, knowing I had had a numinous dream – a dream in which a spiritual teaching is given. I was ecstatic. I had been taught how to respond to my many fears of the outside world. The dream had shown and told me where my true safety lies – within myself, standing next to Jesus, a living symbol of my inner connection to God.

Another way to use dreams in healing fear is to consciously invite a helper to enter your frightening dreams and give you assistance. At your invitation, much emotional healing can take place within the psyche during the dream state. One can heal grievances and emotional wounds. Relationships can be healed. The other person in the relationship does not have to be alive for healing to occur; death and divorce do not stop a relationship.

In the waking dream, our everyday life, one can look for anchors, for something or someone that serves as our lifeline as we pass through and release our fear. The writings of Edgar Cayce suggest reading the Ninety-first Psalm and saying The Lord's Prayer during fearful states. This has the same effect as my Jesus dream, in that these readings serve to reconnect us to our Divine Source. Once that connection is made, we feel safe once again.

I healed my fear of being verbally attacked when speaking in front of a large group by finding an "angel" in the audience, someone who emanated unconditional love and acceptance. When I would become fearful during my speech, I would look at my angel and reconnect to my inner safety. More than once, the person who served as my angel has come forward afterwards and after a loving hug, I have said, "You were my angel," and she has answered, "Yes, I know."

This principle also asks us to bring a peaceful mind into all of our interactions, particularly into an event or interaction that is fearful or stressful. When we bring the energy of peace into conflict we are contributing to the healing of the situation; we are not adding to the pool of negative or fearful energy. One will always feel nurtured if he has handled a troubling situation with equanimity. Equanimity, the evenness of mind, is a balanced state.

In the early 1980's, I was asked to attend a private week-long conference of twenty-one representatives from Egypt, Israel and the United States. The group was comprised of military, political, religious, foreign service, medical and academic leaders. The purpose of the conference, which was held soon after the Camp David talks, was to create a milieu in which differences could be aired, misunderstandings cleared and a sense of brotherhood created. I was asked by one of the major organizers of the conference to sit in a corner of the room and "think peace." He said, " I see you as a battery which can release peace energy into the room. We are going to need as much peaceful energy in the room as possible." So, I sat and thought peace, serving as a "battery" for releasing and intensifying peaceful energies in the room.

When the conference began, I saw its twenty-one members as a large family, one in which there were widely different points of view, many grievances, and a long history of gross misunderstandings. This "family" had spent years resisting any communication and hence any resolution. They distrusted one another tremendously and said so.

They spent the first three days bantering back and forth, voicing accusations and counteraccusations. At the end of the third day, one of the Arabs abruptly stood up, pounded on the table and started shouting very loudly. He felt the conference was a "waste of time" and an insane display of lies and hypocrisy. He threatened to walk out of the room. I saw the man who had invited me to the conference quickly scribbling a note, which to my surprise, was passed to me. I opened the note and read, "Susan, please work harder!!!"

Part of me saw the humor in his request and part of me worked harder and sent more peace into the room. The good news was that the man did not walk out and he did return the next day. From the fourth day on, I witnessed a beautiful demonstration of humanity and brotherhood. The "family" began to resolve their miscommunications. Historical matters related to war and prejudice were explained and clarified. By the seventh and last day, there was a sense of brother-sisterhood in the room. The group had bonded and had joined in purpose to bring more peace into the world by creating peace amongst themselves. This particular group has continued to meet through the years and has continued their bonding as partners in peace.

Another important aspect of this principle is its assurance that we are not alone in our individual quest for inner peace, the first step towards having peace in the world. There are many people in the world who share this vision. These people are the mighty companions who walk with us. As we open our hearts to others, they open their hearts to us. What's true is that peace in the world begins with peace inside us. It's that simple. We each, however, have to make our own choice about wanting or not wanting inner peace. Someday, the peace on the inside will be seen outside in the world as more and more people share this vision of the world. So, it will happen.

WHAT IS MY ATTITUDE?

Contemplate the following questions and write about your feelings in a journal.

1. How intense and pervasive is my fear of the outside world?

2. What relationship do I see between my inner fears and how I live in the world?

3. Have I ever focused on bringing a peaceful self into an unpeaceful situation?

4. To what extent am I trying to create my safety in the world as opposed to within my being?

5. To what extent do I see inner peace as being necessary to outer peace?

6. How much of my day do I experience in a peaceful inner state?

7. Do I have any biases about how inner peace will change my life? Is there a part of me that fears the unknown changes that may occur?

PRACTICING THE PRINCIPLE

Select the exercises that best facilitate and support your healing process, writing your responses in a journal. You may want to prerecord the visualization exercises.

1. Using the technique of dream incubation, request assistance for the healing of your fear, a specific fear or fear in general. I recommend you use the following steps to guide you:

Step 1:   In your journal, state your fear and expand on its many aspects, such as the history of it in your life, how it has controlled you, how it has made decisions for you, how it has manifested in your body, when it seems to occur, how you have dealt with it.

Step 2:   Write the question for your dream self, stating the question simply and to the point. Do not ask many questions, only one succinct one.

Step 3:   Place your journal or paper and pen beside your bed, at easy reach.

Step 4:   Just before falling asleep, say three times, "I will remember my dreams."

Step 5:   Record your dream immediately after you awaken so that it does not slip back into the unconscious.

Work with your dream, following the suggestions given in Chapter Ten.

You might ask someone to facilitate you on your dream. Do not discount any dreams you may have after this request. Even a fragment of a dream can provide insight and direction. You may want to use this technique several times until you gain full cooperation with your dreamer self.

If you had a dream that was fearful and you awoke in the middle of it, sit in silence sometime during the day and complete it as a daydream. Work with the dream in this way until you feel a sense of resolution.

2. Sit in a comfortable position and close your eyes. Take a few deep breaths. Relax. Notice any tension in your body and just relax. Breathe into the tension – breathe out and relax.

Now picture yourself in a place in nature that you experience as being very safe. This can be a place where you have been or you can create a place from your imagination. Find a place that feels totally safe for you. Be there with all your senses, as though you were really there.

If the place does not feel safe, adjust it in some way. Create it as being safe. Add what you need to add. Change what you need to change. Make it an absolutely safe place.

Now stay in that place for the next few minutes. Be there. (Spend about ten minutes in your safe place.)

Gently open your eyes, bringing the consciousness of your safe place back into the room with you. You may want to do a spontaneous drawing of the essence of your safe place. You may want to write in your journal. You may want to contemplate your experience. You may want to share it with someone. Do whatever serves you.

Throughout the day, the week, the month, recall your safe place in times of stress. Focus on bringing the feeling of your safe inner place into your present environment.

3. Sit in silence. Relax your body. Take a few deep breaths.

Imagine a tree of your own choosing appearing in front of you. This is your tree, a tree that you relate to, a tree that relates to you.

Notice what kind of tree it is. Observe its trunk, its branches, its leaves, its size, its height.

Now ever so gently begin to climb the tree. Find a place in the tree that feels comfortable to you. Sit in that place. Allow the tree to support you. Allow the tree to comfort you. Allow yourself to be safe in the tree.

You and the tree now do whatever you want to do. You can stay nuzzled in the tree. You and the tree can go for a walk. You can run and skip. You can dance. Whatever you do, you stay in the tree and the tree carries you safely with it. You and the tree are a joyful pair. Enjoy the joy and support of the tree in whatever way feels right for you. (Do this for about five minutes.)

Now, begin to bring your time with the tree to an end, knowing you can always go back and be with the tree.

When you feel comfortable, open your eyes.

In times of stress, you may want to remember being in your supportive tree and to allow that experience to reconnect you with your inner strength and inner calm.

4. Set as a goal your intention to extend peace in a situation of stress or upset. These opportunities may occur within your home, while driving, in the post office, in the supermarket, in your office.

Whenever you find yourself reacting instead of responding, you know you are not in a state of peace. Shift your intention to thinking and extending peaceful thoughts. You can do this in a similar way as heart-talk (see Chapter Nine).

Observe how your own inner state begins to shift. Do not have expectations of any outside results. Witness them and let them go. Focus only on your own inner thoughts of peace.

5. Think of a way to support yourself during times when you particularly experience fear or expect that you will experience fear. Perhaps having a symbol or an inspirational saying will assist you. It needs to be something that will remind you of your inner safety, your connection to your love essence. Use something that is concrete and that you know will serve you, in the same way that finding an "angel" in an audience served me. Begin to use this symbol and observe any shifts in the intensity of your fear.

6. Continue to strengthen your inner awareness and connection to the Divine Source through regular meditation, contemplation and prayer.

HAVE I HEALED MY ATTITUDE?

After practicing the above exercises, contemplate the following questions and write about your feelings in a journal.

1. Am I more consistent in thinking and extending peaceful thoughts in a stressful situation?

2. Am I feeling more connected to my inner divinity?

3. Do I have a greater sense of being safe within?

4. Do I perceive outer events differently?

5. Have I noticed any shifts in the intensity or pervasiveness of any of my fears?

6. Do I spontaneously call upon the imagery of my safe place or safe tree as a means to reconnect to my place of inner safety?

7. Do I experience any shift in my commitment to bring peace into the world by strengthening my own state of inner peace?

APPLYING THE PRINCIPLE IN SERVICE

This principle more than any other asks you to be an example of one way to live in the world. It asks you to observe when you get caught in the belief that it is the outside world or the body that needs correcting, that needs adjusting. If you are supporting someone whose outer life is in crisis, you will want to be especially vigilant that you don't get swept away in the drama of outer circumstances as holding the secret to the person's inner peace.

As a demonstration teacher of peace, you bring the possibility of inner peace to the supportive relationship. To create this possibility, you need to do your homework – you need to practice your spiritual disciplines and do your inner work so that living a life in peace is a reality.

You will find it helpful to remember that people often express a fear of inner peace. Our minds seem to equate inner peace with passivity, with suddenly becoming a "door mat," with no longer having fun. Quite the opposite is true. When inner peace is experienced, there is tremendous physical, mental and emotional energy available that was not present when the mind was in conflict. Because energy in the psyche is no longer restricted and used to hold conflicts in place, it becomes free and available for use in another way. Whenever energy is unblocked in the human psyche, an elevation in consciousness is experienced. The psyche is more integrated, more flexible, more harmonious. Its parts are in communication with one another. One's outer life is lived from an inner life of happiness, joy and vitality, all symptoms of inner peace.

The inspirational writings of James Allen express the unique contribution of one who is serene while living in the world. He writes:

> Calmness of mind is one of the beautiful jewels of wisdom. It is the result of long and patient effort in self-control. Its presence is an indication of ripened experience, and of a more than ordinary knowledge of the laws and operations of thought.
>
> A man becomes calm in the measure that he understands himself as a thought-evolved being, for such knowledge necessitates the understanding

of others as the result of thought, and as he develops
a right understanding, and sees more and more
clearly the internal relations of things by the action
of cause and effect, he ceases to fuss and fume and
worry and grieve, and remains poised, steadfast,
serene.

The calm man, having learned how to govern himself, knows how to adapt himself to others; and
they, in turn, reverence his spiritual strength, and
feel that they can learn of him and rely upon him.
The more tranquil a man becomes, the greater is his
success, his influence, his power for good.[1]

Inner peace brings with it singleness of purpose, clarity of mind
and strength of character. When you operate from the center of your own
peace, others are drawn to you merely for the comfort of being. We are
all attracted to those who express serenity because their mere presence
appears to reorder our own priorities and bless us with their peace. You
can become this presence for others.

HOW AM I DOING?

Periodically assess your progress in applying this principle in
service to others. Note your concerns, questions and feelings in a journal.

1. Am I bringing more inner peace to my supportive relationships?

2. Do I feel I am more often in a state of inner peace in my personal
   relationships, in my home life and in my work place?

3. Can I more easily recenter myself in stressful situations and
   when I am with the person I am supporting?

4. Do I have a greater sense of equanimity when something
   unexpected happens in the supportive relationship?

5. Does the person I am supporting reflect back to me that he finds
   our supportive relationship emotionally safe?

6. Are more people seeking me out as a source of comfort and support?

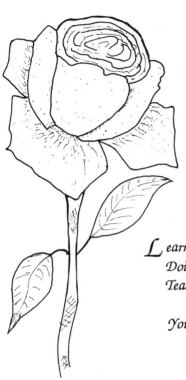

Chapter Thirteen

L earning is finding out what you already know.
Doing is demonstrating that you know it.
Teaching is reminding others that they know
just as well as you.
You are all learners, doers, teachers.

Richard Bach

Principle Nine

WE ARE STUDENTS AND TEACHERS TO EACH OTHER

BASIC TENETS

1. *Every encounter, no matter with whom or what, is a learning opportunity.*

2. *A teacher is anyone who brings a quality to your awareness, either positive or negative, that you have temporarily forgotten was a part of you.*

3. *A teacher provides you with an opportunity to forgive any grievance you have unknowingly been holding against yourself.*

4. *Those people about whom we have the very highest or the very lowest regard are our greatest teachers.*

5. *Teachers and students meet when they are ready to meet; there are no accidents. This is synchronicity.*

6. *Teachers can be found in people, objects, illnesses, accidents, gifts, events, animals, nature, literally anything; in this way the universe is constantly teaching us in a most meaningful way. This is an aspect of synchronicity.*

7. *We are always teaching and we are always learning; we have been given the choice to decide what we wish to teach and what we wish to learn.*

8. *A teacher of healing can be viewed as someone who is temporarily one step ahead of his student.*

9. *A demonstration teacher is someone who teaches others by the example of his life, as though others were observing and learning from his process.*

10. *The universe is generous in that it presents us with multiple and repeated opportunities to learn lessons which guide us to the realization of our true essence.*

THE PRINCIPLE'S MESSAGE

In his later years, Carl Jung, perhaps the most noted analyst of the century, wrote about a principle in the universe which he termed synchronicity. He wrote that at the level of the collective unconscious we are all connected in the universe in a meaningful way, including animate and inanimate objects.[1] Synchronicity illustrates that minds are joined. A concrete example would be to receive a phone call from someone you have just dreamed about or to have a certain person's name on your mind only to learn that the person is ill.

Jungian analyst Jean Bolen wrote in her book *The Tao of Psychology:*

> Synchronicity is the connecting principle (when cause and effect are eliminated by the impossibility of any rational explanation) between our psyches and an external event, in which we feel an uncanny sense of inner and outer being linked. In the experience of a synchronistic event, instead of feeling ourselves to be separated and isolated entities in a vast world we feel the connection to others and the universe at a deep and meaningful level.[2]

Synchronicity plays a major role in the attitudinal healing principle that we are students and teachers to one another. This principle views events that happen and people we meet as learning opportunities that can greatly assist the healing process, should we choose to use them in this way. When people become astutely aware of the emotional and spiritual support the universe provides through synchronicity and work with the symbolism as with a dream, their healing process is accelerated.

Synchronicity can be recognized in one of three ways. It can be a coincidence between a thought or feeling and an outer event. Examples would be wishing you had your own portable computer and within a week someone offers you one, or expressing a desire to go on a certain trip and a distant friend sends you the ticket.

Synchronicity can also take the form of a dream, vision or intuition about an event which in fact is taking place at the same time but in another geographic location. Examples of this form are having a repetitive dream about a relative's family being confused and troubled and later learning that at the very same time you were having the dreams, a son in the family had died unexpectedly, or having the symptoms of a heart attack at the same time your mother is actually having one 3000 miles away.

The third form of synchronicity is a premonition, dream, vision or intuition about something that is going to happen in the future and it does. I remember my grandmother used to suddenly take out the black dress she only wore to funerals and wash and iron it in preparation for the forthcoming death in the family that she sensed. Within a month, such a death would occur.

I first met Clare when she was fourteen years old and have been with her through many years of crisis centering around drug addiction, accidents, family problems, sexual abuse and relationship problems. At age twenty-one and after several accidents which endangered her life, Clare in desperation agreed to take an intensive weekend workshop at the Institute. It was in this workshop that Clare finally released years of anguish and grief and accepted the loving support offered by others.

Soon afterwards, Clare began to see butterflies – butterflies greeted her when she walked out of the front door of her home every morning. Butterflies flew around her wherever she walked. Friends unexpectedly gave her gifts with butterflies on them. She would find butterflies in stores, in windows, wherever she looked. Seen as a symbol of transformation, the butterflies seemed to acknowledge and celebrate Clare's own metamorphosis. They also served as outward reminders for her to practice and reinforce what she had learned. In the company of butterflies, Clare was on her way to a new life.

I encouraged Clare to be aware of events happening around her, knowing that often synchronistic events are especially dramatic after an experience of great emotional intensity. Soon afterwards, she came to see me distressed because a bird had suddenly flown into her car and had been killed. This seemed to trouble Clare very much. We looked at the event synchronistically and worked with it as we would with a dream. When I asked Clare what the bird wanted to say to her after he had been killed, she said, "Here I am flying free and not watching where I am going." In working with this image, Clare saw that her creativity is the part of herself that is like the bird that flies free and because of choices she has made, it is in serious danger of being killed. She shared, "After all those years of using drugs, sex and danger as a way to express my creativity, I must now find new ways. Oh, I hope I have not destroyed my ability to be creative and free in the highest sense." I asked Clare what she had done after her car hit the bird. She responded that she at first had not wanted to look but then had come back and looked at it with much grief and compassion for the value of the bird's life and purpose. I said, "Clare, you'll be all right. You have faced what you have done and have become accountable. You have both regret and compassion for yourself. Now you can move on." And, that she has.

Working with the symbols in our daily life can assist us greatly in our own healing process. Like Clare, every single one of us has this opportunity and can make this choice. Synchronicity is the loving helper from the universe.

I met Sam when I was a graduate student and he was the university chaplain. Sam was a handsome, likeable young man and I fell in love. Sam, however, seemed not to take any interest in me. After graduation, I moved to Alaska where I took my first professional position. With no warning, Sam arrived at my doorstep and asked to marry me. I said no. He got angry. I got angry. He left. He returned. He blamed God. I blamed him. I finally wrote him a scathing letter and he never contacted me again.

Twenty years later when we were both in our forties, Sam and I simultaneously decided to look for one another, to make our peace. Neither of us had any idea about the circumstances or location of the other. Unknown to us (synchronicity comes to the rescue once again!) we had both moved from different parts of the country to Washington, D. C., in the same year.

One morning as I was going up a D. C. metro station escalator and Sam was coming down, our eyes met and we recognized one another. At this point, I had no idea Sam was looking for me and he had no inkling I was looking for him. Sam's first words to me were, "Look, I've had this unbelievable grievance towards you for twenty years. I've allowed my rage at you to affect my life all these years and I don't want this resentment towards you any more. When can we talk about this?"

And so began a series of meetings. At first Sam took the stance of my having unjustly hurt him and I took the view that he was the one with the greater problem. Each of us viewed the other as the victimizer and ourself as the victim. I didn't even remember writing the angry and accusing letter he said I had written. He could quote the letter verbatim and he showed it, worn and torn, to me.

We talked endlessly, speaking the truth about ourselves and what we really felt but hadn't said in the past. We reconstructed our stories and were as honest as we could be but our relationship remained strained. I was getting impatient and feeling more and more that Sam was the one with the problem, not me.

And then, one Monday morning an hour before we were to meet once again, I sat quietly in meditation and in desperation said, "Dear God, let me see what is going on here!" Suddenly a thought came to me, "Susan, you have forgotten – Sam is your brother."

In that instant, I saw that I had been holding Sam out of my heart as a way to cope with my emotional pain regarding our situation. I had stopped seeing him as a fellow human being with his own unique purpose and contribution. I survived what I now realized had been a painful experience for me by pushing the pain away and denying it all these years. I had felt guilty about what I had done and projected the problem onto Sam.

When Sam came that morning, I acknowledged to him that I now saw that for twenty years I had handled my pain in our relationship by closing him out of my heart, by closing him out of the human race. I knew now that I carried great guilt about doing that. I told him that now I truly saw him as my brother, that I saw him as another beautiful soul on earth who was moving through his life and who had a right to be here. I took responsibility for what I had thought all these years. I became accountable.

Sam surprised me by bursting into tears and saying, "Those are the very words I have been waiting twenty years to hear from you." All conflict melted between us. Our learning together was complete.

Sam and I had been students and teachers to each other. From Sam, I learned that I had denied my guilt and then projected it onto him in the form of anger, thereby making him a victimizer and me the victim. Sam's gift to me was his persistence and insistence in working on our relationship until, as he said, "I can be free of my resentment of you." Any time we separate ourselves from another by refusing to see our shared humanity, we will feel guilty. The Indian saint Maharaji used to say, "Don't put anyone out of your heart," to which Stephen Levine has added, "Because when you put someone out of your heart, you remove yourself as well."[3] I had not only put Sam out of my heart, I had put myself out as well.

My gift to Sam as a teacher is Sam's story, one he may or may not ever share with me. Sam presently is minister of a church that I have driven past daily for four years; as I pass I thank him and wish him well. We have yet to meet again.

The most significant teachers in our lives are usually people with whom we have primary relationships, such as parents, siblings, children and spouses. Because these relationships are lifelong, they provide us with opportunity after opportunity to learn forgiveness and unconditional love. Death and divorce do not stop a relationship. We can continue to view someone who has died or our former spouse as offering learning opportunities.

Learning from a relationship does not necessarily mean staying in it. There are no hard and fast rules about what to do in a troubled relationship. The purpose of any relationship is to learn what it has to offer. A person can be a demonstration teacher of various qualities, or of the nature of the healing process itself. Also, a person can serve to trigger within us a negative reaction, a negative quality which we need to acknowledge within ourself and forgive.

Demonstration teachers are those people who teach the healing or transformational process through the example of their own lives. We often learn more by observing how people respond in a certain situation or how they live their lives than by any great philosophical teachings they might espouse. A demonstration teacher can be a guide, a helper along the way, someone who takes our hand and leads us through a difficult time. Such a teacher is someone who may show us the contrast of choosing a life of suffering or a life of joy. Their very life may be a demonstration of one of these choices. It is important to identify the demonstration teachers in our own life and to allow ourselves to learn from them. That is their gift to us.

One of my most memorable demonstration teachers was a woman I only met once. What she came to teach me was the effects of choosing bitterness, resentment and hatred as opposed to choosing forgiveness. She called and asked to see me for a counseling session. Her former husband had taken one of my workshops and had spoken of me. She wanted to talk with me about some matters in her own life. When she walked in, she said, "How dare you help my husband! He has betrayed me, he has betrayed his children, he has gone off with other women, he is into this crazy spiritual stuff. And he said you helped him. How dare you help him. He doesn't deserve it!" From that opening statement came her story of great emotional pain about a marriage that was disrupted by betrayal of all forms. For ten years she had been harboring this pain and as I looked at her, I saw the anguish on her face and the bitterness in her eyes. She revealed she was an alcoholic, had no friends and no sense of purpose in her life.

She was telling my story! Our marriage stories were almost identical. The day she came for the appointment, August 10, was the tenth anniversary of the day I mentally marked as being the day my own marriage had collapsed. The universe's anniversary gift was someone who symbolized a choice that I, myself, could have made. I saw the effects of the choice of ten years of bitterness and unforgiveness. I knew how close I had come to making the same choice as this woman. On that day I renewed the commitment to my own healing process and I held great compassion for the part of me that this woman represented. She demonstrated by her life a powerful teaching for me and I will always deeply acknowledge her for that.

WHAT IS MY ATTITUDE?

Contemplate the following questions and write about your feelings in a journal.

1. To what extent do I view everyone and everything that enters my life as a potential teacher for me?

2. In what ways do I serve as a teacher to others?

3. Am I aware of demonstration teachers in my life?

4. How able am I to see beyond appearances to another level of truth?

5. Am I aware of the principle of synchronicity in my life?

6. When in my life have I been particularly aware of synchronistic events?

7. Have I made a choice as to what it is I would truly want to teach in this life and what it is I want to learn?

PRACTICING THE PRINCIPLE

Select the exercises that best facilitate and support your healing process, writing your responses in a journal. You may want to prerecord the visualization exercises.

1. List the people in your life that you feel have served or are now serving as demonstration teachers. Next to their names, write a few words as to what it is you feel you are learning from them.

2. Write down an event that you have recently experienced and have identified as synchronistic. Work with it as you would a dream, asking yourself the following questions:

- What feelings did I experience during the synchronistic event and afterwards?

- What commentary might the event be making on my current life?

- Does the event seem to comment on a decision I have made or an experience I have recently had?

- Is the event alerting me in some way to something I have an opportunity to pay closer attention to, to make a choice about or to affirm?

- What specifically do I feel this event is teaching me?

Select the key players, events, animals, objects or qualities of the event and speak as though you are them. Write down the message each has to give you. Carry on a dialogue between yourself and the various parts of the event.

3. Do the same process in #2 but select an event in your life that does not seem synchronistic but can be defined more as being distressing, anxiety-producing or uncomfortable, something you do not have a good feeling about.

4. Select a past or present relationship about which you feel conflict or uneasiness. This person can be living or dead. Write the person's

name at the top of a blank sheet of paper. On the left-hand side of the page list all of the negative feelings and qualities that this person seems to trigger for you. Be as complete as you can.

Across from each negative quality, write its opposite in the form of a value. For example, if you have written "won't tell me how he feels" you might write "the value of communication" as its opposite. If you have written "is only concerned with material goods" you might write "the value of spiritual growth."

After you have completed your lists, circle those values that you feel this person has most served to teach you.

At the end of the paper, write a brief thank you note to this person. If it feels appropriate you may even want to mail it. Since minds are joined, offering the thought of healing to the universe will also be effective.

5. You are going to draw what is called a "lifeline." The following is an example:

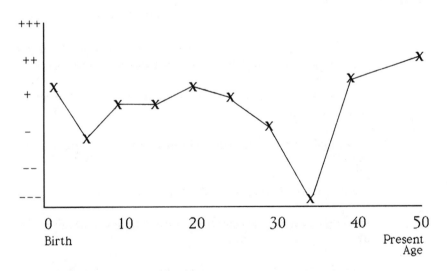

The bottom line indicates the number of years you have lived thus far, beginning at "0" to indicate birth and marking intervals of 5 or 10 years after that point until your present age.

On the left side of the graph, you find indices of how you recall those years as being, with --- representing three minuses or very negative, all the way up to the very positive +++. As you review your life, draw a line which reflects these positive and negative times. You may recall specific events of your suffering and specific events of joy.

For example, my lifeline as depicted in the above chart shows a + mark at the time of my birth. I made this mark because I was a wanted child and there were several positive omens that occurred around the time of my birth which made my parents very happy. The first significant dip occurs at age five, when my mother suffered a postpartum depression after the birth of my sister. At this age, I experienced losing my mother emotionally. My early school years went well but at age seven I was sexually abused by my grandfather; this event created much pain for the family and for myself. As my life continued, you can see I experienced events that were both positive and troubling. At age thirty-five, I became severely depressed. Since that time, however, I have gradually experienced much healing and I have felt increasingly positive about my life.

Now do your own chart. Take your time as you reflect on the events of your life and how they affected you at the time. If you have no conscious memory of what a certain age was like for you, mark what intuitively feels right.

After you complete the chart, ask yourself the following questions:

• What did I learn from the various events of my life, both the ones I experienced as painful and the ones that brought me joy?

• Do I see any patterns in my life, like a certain kind of event repeating itself?

• Can I look at my chart without judgement or disapproval of myself?

• What has my life taught me thus far?

• How do I currently feel about my life and how would I describe it?

• How do I imagine my life line will look in future years?

6. Reread Chapter Seven. Compare and contrast the principle, WE ARE STUDENTS AND TEACHERS TO EACH OTHER to the principle, GIVING AND RECEIVING ARE THE SAME.

HAVE I HEALED MY ATTITUDE?

After practicing the above exercises, contemplate the following questions and write about your feelings in a journal.

1. Does being in this world feel any more purposeful or meaningful to me?

2. Am I more aware of synchronistic events and their messages?

3. Am I more aware of the kind of teacher that I am to others?

4. Am I better able to view events as learning opportunities and less as unrelated events that happen in my life?

5. Have I made a new choice about what it is I would like to teach others and therefore what it is I want to nurture and cultivate within myself?

6. Have my feelings changed towards those people whom I perceive as triggering emotional pain for me? In what ways?

7. Am I viewing my life and its learning more as a process than as having a specific end result?

APPLYING THE PRINCIPLE IN SERVICE

A supportive relationship within the context of this principle is one in which both individuals have an opportunity to learn from one another. As a facilitator, you may discover that you have a similar life story to the person you are supporting. You have an opportunity to view your own story from your Witness Self and thereby gain a different perspective. You will probably gain new insights about your own life issues. The opportunity may also arise for you to deepen your understanding of what a supportive relationship is and how its form may vary from person to person.

I became a facilitator for Rochelle when she was experiencing her third bout with cancer. When she called our Institute and requested support, she said that the first time she had cancer, she took a physical approach. The second time she said she took a psychological approach and now she wanted a spiritual approach. Because she was quite ill, I met with Rochelle in her home. Rochelle was a vivacious woman who happened to be exactly my age and in the prime of life. She had just helped start a new art museum and led what she described as a full and vibrant life. Everything about Rochelle was dashing – her glamorous appearance, her flare for the dramatic, her taste in art, her love for elegant living and dining.

When asked what kind of supportive relationship she wanted, she said she just wanted me to listen and not "vie for my time." And so, I did. Rochelle shared her concerns about her children, finances, family and her work. She expressed worries about not believing there was life after death. She did not want to hear one word about my point of view about anything or about my own life experiences. At the end of my weekly visits to her home, she would simply say, "Oh, thank you for not vying for my time. This is the only time in my week when no one is vying for my time and being with you is my time."

Rochelle surprised me at the end of one of our meetings near the end of her life when she asked what I thought happened after death. I shared my views but Rochelle readily discounted them. Still, she talked often of her feelings about her own death.

During our last visit together as Rochelle was near death, she suddenly said to me, "Well, Susan, it took me a while but now I think I finally know why you've been my support person. It was so I could catch inner peace from you!"

I know I "caught" a great deal from Rochelle as she was a wonderful teacher for me. Because we were so similar in age, Rochelle forced me for the first time to confront my feelings about my own death. She also taught me that sharing one's own views or personal stories is not always a supportive thing to do. To serve Rochelle, I needed to be there totally for her, listening and listening, giving her total and undivided attention and not "vying for her time."

Sometimes the person you are supporting may seem to "push your buttons." Angers, fears or doubts may be triggered by the person you are supporting. In the context of this principle, such a dynamic asks that you examine your reaction, noting whether it represents a grievance you are unknowingly holding against yourself or another person. The person you are supporting may in some way remind you of some facet of yourself or of an unhealed relationship. If so, you will need to work on these issues outside of the supportive relationship in order to be fully present for the person you are supporting.

HOW AM I DOING?

Periodically assess your progress in applying this principle in service to others. Note your concerns, questions and feelings in a journal.

1. Do I see my relationship with the person I am supporting as a learning opportunity for each of us?

2. Do I use my Witness Self when I am supporting someone?

3. Do I take responsible action when the person I am supporting "pushes my button" by examining the source of my upset and doing some inner work concerning it?

4. Do I spend time contemplating the nature of our supportive relationship?

5. Am I aware of effective communication skills when I am facilitating, being alert to the appropriateness and value of whether or not to share my own story or my own experiences?

6. Is the relationship a nurturing one for both of us?

7. Do I feel open to inner direction when I am with the person I am supporting?

8. When I am supporting someone, am I aware of how this principle relates to the principle, GIVING AND RECEIVING ARE THE SAME?

Chapter Fourteen

T he mark of your ignorance is the depth
of your belief in injustice and tragedy.
What the caterpillar calls the end of the world,
The master calls a butterfly.

Richard Bach

Principle Ten

WE CAN FOCUS ON THE WHOLE OF LIFE RATHER THAN THE FRAGMENTS

BASIC TENETS

1. *When we focus on the whole of life, we recognize fragments but do not identify with them. We identify with the whole, which is a spiritual perspective.*

2. *The whole of life includes the fragments but is not the fragments.*

3. *Focusing on the whole of life means seeing beyond appearances. It is seeing Oneness in duality, Unity in diversity.*

4. *The function of the Witness Self is to be aware of the whole of life.*

5. *Focusing on the whole of life is living life fully and with joy.*

6. *The whole of life reflects the integration and balance of one's spiritual, mental, emotional and physical selves.*

7. *The ability to see life as a whole is strengthened through meditation and spiritual disciplines.*

8. *The Higher Self is concerned with the whole of life; the lower self is concerned with the fragments.*

199

9. *Fragments are those thoughts, desires, feelings, activities and things that distract us from the awareness of the whole of life.*

10. *A thought, desire, feeling or activity becomes a fragment when we identify with it and see it as our salvation. Fragments are attachments.*

THE PRINCIPLE'S MESSAGE

This principle masterfully adjusts our personal and our world vision. We no longer see our lives or the world as made up of meaningless and isolated events and happenings. Rather, we see ourselves and the world as interrelated and bonded by humanity. Astronauts remind us that the planet is a living organism that functions as a single unit. The astronauts describe the earth as a single beautiful, elegant blue jewel suspended in space. Even though multiple events are occurring on earth with great fury and rapidity, the earth looks serene and whole when seen from afar.

So it is with each of us. When we see isolated events, thoughts, ideas, desires, emotions and material goods in our lives from a spiritual perspective, we see the whole of life. Our life contains the parts, the fragments, but we are not these fragments. We are more than that. We can be likened to the serene and beautiful jewel of earth seen from afar.

The yearning to experience the whole of who we are is strong within each of us. When we hear beautiful music, see a breathtaking view of the mountains or the ocean or hold and comfort a loved one, we get a glimpse of the exquisite beauty of our wholeness. To the extent that we have lost sight of this wholeness, we will experience our life as purposeless, meaningless and hopeless.

Clare, the twenty-one-year-old college senior, whose transformative experience in one of the Institute's workshops was accompanied by the synchronistic appearance of butterflies, wrote me after her experience. She wrote about the emotional pain she experienced when she desperately sought meaning in life's fragments. When Clare was able to let go of her past, she made an inward spiritual shift and reconnected with her Higher Self. She suddenly experienced the reality of the whole of life. With Clare's permission, I share her letter.

Dear Susan,

I am a warrior. Anyone who seeks the truth instead of running in fear is a warrior. The truth is not easy to find. Sometimes, great loss or pain or near-death experiences are necessary forces in changing one's vision.

In my case, two elements were at work simultaneously. The first was that I tried any and every escape imaginable. The second was the intensity with which I ran. Together, thank God, they brought my life to a turning point. I will never be the same person again.

My absorption with fragments began when I was four years old and started running from my home life. I remember staying out with friends as late and as often as possible. My mother was very depressed, addicted to Valium and suicidal; my father was six thousand miles away. My stepfather was a Hungarian refugee whose career with the U.S. Army had left neither his psyche nor his heart unscathed.

Adding to my pain was the neighbor's son. I'll never forget him. He was about twenty-years-old, stood six feet three inches, weighed about 350 pounds, and always smelled badly. I think he was slightly retarded. Frank abused me sexually from the time I was four until I was about seven years of age.

We moved to Hawaii for four years and then back to the Washington, D.C., area, where I would spend the next ten years. The race accelerated. My early schooling exceeded that of my new peers by a couple of years. This both pleased and distracted my parents and teachers. I was also the best athlete in the school. When competitions arose, I broke every record there was to break. Once again, this made me popular with parents, teachers and now peers. I had everyone convinced that my life was beautiful, and above all, that I was living it correctly.

However, by the age of eight, I was smoking cigarettes and drinking alcohol; by nine, I was smoking marijuana and, by ten, I was arrested for theft. This does not refer to the conventional childhood lifting of candy, gum or small toys at the grocery. I took a screwdriver, then caught a bus to the nearest parking garage and began stealing parts off cars. For the next thirteen years, my acting-out behaviors, habits and addictions increased in variety and severity.

By the age of twelve, I was heavily engaged in sex, having

202 TO SEE DIFFERENTLY

intercourse with males and females of all races, ages and disposi-
tions. We did it in almost every way and combination possible. A
great deal of my secret life was assisted by a wonderful tree outside
my bedroom window. This tree proved to be a literal vehicle of
escape. My daily routine consisted of running all day, whether
attending or skipping school, then staying away until dinner time.
After dinner I would run again until my ten o'clock bedtime. When
the clock struck midnight, I would climb out my bedroom window
and down the tree. My older friends (I always had friends much,
much older than myself) would be waiting in their cars. Our
adventures began by 'sparking up' a joint and kicking back a few
beers. After we had a nice high going, we embarked on our
midnight excursions to swimming pools, bars and night clubs – all
of which were accompanied by sex, sex, and more sex!

At this point it is necessary to clarify the extent of my
substance abuse. It was beyond the recreational; it was obsessive.
I was nine years old the first time I got drunk. From junior high on,
marijuana, cigarettes and alcohol were almost always daily events.
Cocaine usage was frequent; it went up my nose, in my mouth,
eyes, lungs and even in my veins. I also distracted myself with:
LSD, PCP, speed, opium, Valium, codeine, Percodan, Demerol,
nitrous oxide, hallucinogenic mushrooms and hashish as much
and as frequently as possible. Again, my popularity with people
ensured an ongoing supply of numerous substances to ingest in
creative combinations.

It's a miracle I am still here. I realize now that part of this
miracle was my mother's continual love, prayers and support. I
now know what a lifeline she provided. She was the one who
brought me to you, remember? Her own healing and spiritual
growth over the past ten years have been instrumental in my
survival and now serve as a model for me.

The extent of my desire to block out pain during all those
years, however, led me to the ultimate escape – suicide attempts.
While I never consciously tried to kill myself, subconsciously I
engaged in life-threatening situations repeatedly. One such example was a terrible car accident. I was high and turned off the
headlights of my mother's car on a narrow, curvy road, and hit a
tree head-on. The car was totaled, and my friend and I severely
injured. The chief of staff in the emergency room gave me a very
clear, loud message: she took my hand, looked me in the eye and
told me I was VERY, VERY LUCKY. She was right. Although I

heard her words, I was not able to make the necessary changes. This was just the first of several such episodes which included a gun barrel in my mouth, a sixty-foot leap from a cliff, and stockpiled pills and razor blades. Not only did I choose life-threatening situations, they chose me. I was assaulted and raped. I had an abortion. A stove blew up and my clothes caught fire. I was caught in a vortex of disaster.

Of all the fragments I've explored, athletics is the only productive one I've used. Using my body with the same unbridled intensity used for everything else gave me physical and emotional strength. I began with gymnastics in the third grade. Although by the age of twelve my gymnastic ability merited consideration for Olympic training, I became 'bored' and quit to maintain my social antics. Soccer and basketball provided a physical outlet and opportunity to excel, yet allowed time for drugs and sex. My soccer ability led to numerous college scholarship offers. In my spare time, I also participated in organized swimming and diving, cross-country running, volleyball and tackle football (I was the only girl in the league). Most recently I've been involved in water skiing and competitive body building. Despite the merits of athletics, I used them as yet another means to distract and fragment my life.

Many of us try to skirt the issue of our own problem solving. Yet from my own experiences I have come to the conclusion that the running itself generates great pain mentally, physically and especially, spiritually. This past year has been almost unbearable. My methods of escaping were so severe that I was just shy of doing myself in. At the same time this was a necessary period. All the pain I experienced caused me to seek a new answer. None of my old answers were working any longer – not even momentarily. So, I decided to stop running and face my entire life history.

This summer marked the beginning of the change that was to take place in my life. The first step in this transition began with the Level I workshop held at the Institute. Level I provided me with a sense of camaraderie in my search for the truth. I listened to many people cry because of their pain – pain which was generated by fragmented life styles. Of course, everyone's story was unique. However, there were definitely commonalities amongst us all. Unknowingly, this workshop greatly heightened my awareness about my own struggles both mentally and spiritually. For the first time in my life I acknowledged all my pain, anger, rage, guilt, abuse, fear and sorrows. All of this was necessary for me to attend another workshop at the Institute, Level II.

In the Level II workshop I realized that I carried tremendous guilt for all my past actions. Because of this guilt I was tremendously self-destructive. In turn, self-destruction created more guilt. The cycle was self-supporting and unending. The key to my freedom was forgiveness. I had to forgive myself in order to allow myself to heal. That's exactly what I did in the workshop.

At one point during my personal work I was sobbing uncontrollably and couldn't hold my head or body up. I felt so overwhelmed and burdened that I wanted to give in to my guilt. I felt I couldn't continue. However, at just that moment, you whispered softly in my ear, "Clare, you are a warrior. Remember, Clare, you are a warrior." These words had a tremendous impact on me. Suddenly I felt connected with my Higher Self and empowered to transcend my guilt. My back felt strong again and the emotional and spiritual strength was there for me to continue the process of my own forgiveness. I knew I WAS GOING TO MAKE IT.

Acknowledging all that I did, I then forgave myself. A beautiful metamorphosis had occurred. I was reborn. By consciously facing my entire past I broke through my separation from my Higher Self.

I now see the truth and therefore have no need to fragment my life any longer. I am now focusing on the whole of life. It feels wonderful.

I love you – and the new me,

Clare

Clare's story is an example of the warrior courage needed in healing. Once assured of this courage, she accepted the unconditional emotional support provided in the loving safe space created by the workshop participants. She was able to confront and transcend her guilt and shame because she no longer felt emotionally and spiritually abandoned by others and by a Higher Power.

Guilt and shame are forms of fear resulting from the emotional and spiritual abandonment of the child by the parents and the belief that one has been abandoned by the Divine Source. One can also abandon his spiritual self by believing he has separated himself from the Divine

Source. He senses that he has done something wrong and therefore deserves to be punished. He feels guilty. Believing himself to be inherently unworthy and inadequate, he feels humiliated, belittled, devalued and powerless. He feels shame.

Feelings of guilt and shame become addictive – the more guilt and shame a person feels, the more he abuses himself or others and the more guilt and shame he feels. The more guilt and shame he feels, the more he feels emotionally and spiritually separated from others and from the Divine Source. The more he feels separated, the more he feels he has done something wrong and should be punished. He uses defenses of fighting, freezing or fleeing to protect himself emotionally. These defenses make him unreachable and isolated and perpetuate the feelings of separation and thus of worthlessness.

Addictions, whether it be to drugs, material goods, food, money, sex or thoughts of worthlessness are one's attempt in the physical world to reconnect to the Divine Source and therefore to one's worth and value, to one's emotional and spiritual selves. Jungian analyst Robert Johnson writes,

> Addiction is the negative side of spiritual seeking. We are looking for an exultation of the spirit; but instead of fulfillment we get a short-lived physical thrill that can never satisfy the chronic, gnawing emptiness with which we are beset.[1]

When guilt and shame are shared openly and honestly with at least one trusted person, the psychic energy used to hold on to this fear of worthlessness is released and the fear is transcended. The sense of guilt and shame, of being inherently unworthy and inadequate and of deserving punishment, dissolves. In its place is a reconnection to the Divine Source and to one's sense of self-worth. One is then able to shift to a focus on the whole of life rather than the fragments.

WHAT IS MY ATTITUDE?

Contemplate the following questions and write about your feelings in a journal.

  1. What are the fragments in my life and to what extent do I feel identified with them?

2. When in my life have I especially experienced the whole of life?

3. What does it mean "to focus on" the whole of life?

4. What does "looking beyond appearances" mean to me? Am I aware of searching for the truth beyond appearances?

5. Am I aware of using my Witness Self to observe the fragments in my life?

6. Do I feel aware of my spirituality?

7. How am I specifically strengthening my ability to see life as a whole?

PRACTICING THE PRINCIPLE

Select the exercises that best facilitate and support your healing process, writing your responses in a journal. You may want to prerecord the visualization exercises.

1. On a blank sheet of paper, make three columns, one titled Physical, another Mental, another Emotional. Under each title, list what you feel are fragments in your life that distract you from your spiritual self. Place your awareness in your Witness Self in order to do this exercise without feelings of guilt or shame. Just observe your fragments. Attempt to be as complete and specific with your lists as you can. You may want to begin the lists and then return to them to add more items before continuing the next part of the exercise, which is similar to Exercise 5 in Chapter Ten.

Either to yourself aloud or to a trusted friend say, for each item, "I forgive myself for_____, I forgive myself for_____, I forgive myself for_____" until you have completed the three lists. Observe your reaction to doing this and if tears come, let them come.

If you do this exercise with a trusted friend, have him look into your eyes and say, "you are forgiven" after each item. You may also want to complete the exercise by sharing with this friend, "I acknowledge myself for _____, I acknowledge myself for _____ ." Again, be as specific as you can as to certain events, feelings or attitudes. If you do this exercise alone, write down and then say aloud, I acknowledge myself for_____, I acknowledge myself for_____, I acknowledge myself for_____ ." Continue the acknowledgements until you have a sense of completion.

Conclude the exercise with an activity that is comforting and reassuring to you, like listening to music that uplifts your spirits, going for a walk in nature, meditating or reading inspirational material.

2. In your journal begin to make a list of affirmations that specifically serve to reinforce your awareness of your wholeness. Add to this list daily. Examples of such affirmations are:

> I am willing to accept love.
> I am not alone.
> I am one with God and the universe.
> I am whole and good.
> I am deserving of unconditional love.
> I honor my process of healing.
> I will accept one compliment today and hold it in my
>   heart and allow it to nurture me.
> I am okay and if I am not okay, that is okay, too.

3. With your journal in hand, go outdoors and find a tree that especially speaks to you. Write a dialogue with the tree, as though you are carrying on a conversation with it. Trees are symbols of wisdom, of wholeness. Therefore, by communicating with a tree, you can connect to the wholeness within yourself. The following is a sample of such a dialogue, shared with permission from its author, Renée Schlessinger.

> Renée: Dogwood, I've always had a love for your delicate and beautiful petals. I'm aware that I barely even know you exist the rest of the year but I would definitely want to get better acquainted.

> Dogwood Tree: Thank you for noticing. I am not one of the big,

bold statuesque trees you see in the woods but I'm able to grow and survive with very little soil, sun or space and I can be graceful about it. I don't let my branches shade or kill the grass or other vegetation. I get by with the fewest of limbs for my nourishment.

Renée: Yes, I feel that is what attracts me to you – your simplicity of life, and also how you bend all your limbs to one side to get out of the way of that other stronger flowering tree next to you. You do look fragile but that is just to the inexperienced eye. I now can see you are as determined to live and show your beauty as any other; yet you know you don't have to hurt or be hurt by other forms.

Dogwood Tree: Yes, it is challenging to survive sometimes and not confront our overbearing neighbors. But I guess I like the challenge and I believe it is not only important, but essential.

Renée: Don't you feel like getting even with some of the larger, stronger trees that want to take your space and life?

Dogwood Tree: Sometimes I wish I were a lot bigger and stronger, but when my blossoms are ready to come out, I see all my patience and adaptability pay off, when everyone really appreciates my inner beauty. You needn't be the largest, strongest or smartest to find your perfect space. Just live each day to the best of your ability.

Renée: I guess I recently was feeling my space being threatened.

Dogwood Tree: Look at one of my flowers.

Renée: Yes, I see it.

Dogwood Tree: Each one is as beautiful as the next in its own way. If I had room around my north side to have branches and flowers, would that change what you admire in that single beautiful flower?

Renée: No – I see. I can grow and develop the same beauty in my limited space. I needn't be deterred by other objects along my path. Thank you, Dogwood Tree, for your wisdom!

Dogwood Tree: You're welcome!

4. In silence and with your eyes closed, imagine the little child within you that has been emotionally wounded. Particularly note whether your inner child feels any shame or guilt, if he has felt hurt and humiliated in any way as he was growing up.

Think of him as your own child. Support him, hold him. Reassure him of your love for him. Imagine how you would relate to him in his pain. If he wants to take some emotional risks (like crying or throwing a temper tantrum), support him in doing that.

Assure your inner child that you will always honor him and that you will always be aware of his presence and his value. Then make him about the size of a thimble and put him lovingly in your heart. Imagine him sitting in your heart with great joy and safety. Go about your daily activities knowing that this precious part of you is with you always.

5. Imagine yourself as an astronaut out in space looking back at Earth. Be aware that you have taken only yourself and a small and efficient spaceship with you. What does Earth look like? See its beauty, its glory as it is suspended in space.

Become aware of what has happened and is happening on Earth, on its lands, in its seas and in its atmospheres. Become aware of what has happened in your own personal life while residing there. Be complete with the description of Earth as it is and as you live your life on it.

Place your awareness in your heart. From your heart, from your compassionate and loving self, what do you say to planet Earth? What wisdom and understanding is in your heart about your home on Earth? What do you say to her? What do you say to the people, the animals, the oceans, the land, the skies? What is the purpose of Earth? What is her function? How is she doing? What does she need? What does she want? What is your function on Earth? How are you going to help her out? What awarenesses, choices or values do you want to bring back to her upon your return from space? Be specific and simple. A small step, perhaps.

When you are ready, bring yourself back to Earth. Bring into reality the step you want to take, for yourself, for Mother Earth.

6. Whenever you find yourself entangled in a physical, mental or emotional fragment and cannot see beyond appearances, repeat this brief dis-identification exercise until you feel a shift in your awareness.

> I have a body, but I am not my body.
> I am the one who is aware.
>
> I have emotions, but I am not my emotions.
> I am the one who is aware.
>
> I have thoughts, but I am not my thoughts.
> I am the one who is aware.
>
> I have desires, but I am not my desires.
> I am the one who is aware.
>
> I have _____ (the fragment) but I am
>   not _____ (the fragment).
> I am the one who is aware.
>
> I am the centered I, the Wise Inner Self.
> I am the center of pure consciousness.

7. Reread Chapter Three as a way to reinforce your understanding of the healing process.

HAVE I HEALED MY ATTITUDE?

After practicing the above exercises, contemplate the following questions and write about your feelings in a journal.

1. Am I more aware of what fragments are present in my life and is it easier for me to dis-identify from them?

2. Do I have a greater sense of myself as a part of the whole of humanity?

3. Do I have a clearer sense of what it means to look beyond appearances?

4. Has my awareness of my spiritual reality strengthened? Do I feel in more communication with that part of myself?

5. Do I more easily see the positive possibilities in a situation than I used to?

6. Do I better understand the role guilt and shame have played in my life?

7. Do I have a greater sense of my own self-worth and value?

APPLYING THE PRINCIPLE IN SERVICE

The whole of life includes the fragments. When you are focused on the whole of life, you recognize the fragments but do not identify with them. You identify instead with your spiritual reality. Within the supportive relationship you need to strive to stay focused in this reality. If you lose yourself in either your own or another person's fragment, you become part of the problem rather than the solution. It is like seeing the trees and not the forest, like seeing the clouds but not the sky.

As a facilitator, you have compassion for the person's experiences by joining with him in working through the issue, not by joining with and becoming part of the problem. When you join the problem of another, the problem becomes more solid and less solvable. You reinforce or strengthen the fragment's reality. Going over and over the problem obsessively reinforces it and you will get "stuck" in it. This is like continuing to accelerate the car once it is stuck in the mud. The car gets increasingly stuck in ever deeper mud. What is needed is another approach and a helping hand. If the helper gets in the car and continues to accelerate it, it will not help. The car will only go deeper. The problem will still be there. The helper joins in searching for a way to get "unstuck." And when the car is freed, the helper sends it on its way.

So it is when facilitating someone. You offer a helping hand to assist the person in detaching from the fragment, in getting unstuck. You join the person in finding a way to see the fragment differently. The person is empowered. He is the driver of his car and he is free to continue his journey. Perhaps once outside the mud, he sees the reason he got stuck. He doesn't have to get stuck again. But if he does, he now knows there are ways to get unstuck. If necessary, he can ask for a helping hand or, as is often the case, a helping hand finds him.

Successfully moving through the three major stages of personal development will result in your being able to support someone from a perspective of the whole of life. In the first stage, you gather life experiences and acquire perceptions of them. These experiences and perceptions are internalized and become part of your psychological makeup. In the second stage, you glean what you have learned from your experiences and the perceptions of experiences. Emotional wounds and perceptions are healed. Finally, you share lessons learned and your healing with others. Although these stages interface with one another throughout life, there are identifiable hallmarks in each of them.

Stage One: Acquiring life experiences

Very early in life you begin to acquire experiences and perceptions about your experiences. You collect a wide range of isolated yet inter-related perceptions about life and make certain choices about how to live and view life. Your life takes on its own unique hue, its own flavor. Outer events are important in this stage and you tend to see these as the source of meaning and purpose. This period spans from birth throughout life, with the major portion occurring before the age of thirty-five. It is possible to stay in this stage throughout a lifetime. Such a person spends his life collecting experiences from the outer world and creating his view of the world's reality. Clare focused intently on this stage. In her short twenty-one years, she experienced multiple aspects of the material and physical world.

Stage Two: Integrating and healing life experiences

In this stage you begin to question the meaning of your life experiences and to confront unresolved emotional issues. Although this stage can begin at any time, it usually does not occur with much intensity until one is at least thirty-five years of age. In this stage, you begin to shift from being outward-oriented to being inward-directed. Depending upon the severity of early childhood trauma, you may spend considerable time focusing on this stage. It is in this stage that you confront your attachments and identifications with the fragments of life and begin to shift to the whole of life. To become a healed healer, you must move through this stage with commitment and thoroughness. You must shed your swallowed tears, deliver undelivered communications, externalize fear and own all parts of yourself.

Stage Three: Sharing life experiences

When you have moved through Stage Two to Stage Three, you share the wisdom gleaned from your life experiences and share your healed mind. You create and hold a space for others to be healed of conditions which have been healed within yourself. As Clare is healed of her addictions, guilt, shame and sexual abuse, she will hold a tremendously large space for the possibility of healing those with similar histories.

A person bypassing Stage Two will also share his life experiences and wisdom with others but it will be through a veil of the unhealed and unintegrated self. Those who bypass Stage Two usually seek to have their needs met through others as they have not had them met within themselves.

Although these stages occur somewhat sequentially, they interrelate and communicate with one another throughout life. As you are healed, you will have more and more healing energy to give in serving others. Circumstances continue to occur throughout life that provide opportunities for learning and healing. As you serve others, you are served.

As you move through the three stages with commitment and integrity you will emanate your healing through your peacefulness and joy. You will be able to set aside your own issues and be totally present for the person you are supporting. You will become increasingly adept at seeing beyond appearances and maintaining your focus on the whole of life through your own continued inner work and spiritual disciplines. Your unique way of being of service to others will continue to broaden and deepen.

HOW AM I DOING?

Periodically assess your progress in applying this principle in service to others. Note your concerns, questions and feelings in a journal.

1. Am I identifying less with the fragments of my own life when I am supporting someone?

2. Can I view the person I am supporting beyond his fragmented life?

3. Am I more present with a person and less distracted by my thoughts, my own personal story and my judgements?

4. Am I able to see another perspective of a situation beyond what appears to be?

5. Do I more clearly see how my own life experiences enrich my support of another?

6. Am I more conscious of moving through the three stages and do I see how they interface in my own life?

7. How do I feel about the way in which I extend a helping hand? Do I feel I am able to create a space in which the person I am supporting feels empowered?

Chapter Fifteen

*I f the doors of perception were cleansed,
everything would appear to man
as it is, infinite.*

William Blake

Principle Eleven

SINCE LOVE IS ETERNAL, DEATH NEED NOT BE VIEWED AS FEARFUL

BASIC TENETS

1. *We have a body but we are not our bodies. We are more than that. We are the Self.*

2. *Fear of death equals fear of life.*

3. *Without the fear of death, one can live fully in his love essence.*

4. *The body dies but the spirit, the love essence, does not.*

5. *Dying and death are learning opportunities.*

6. *Quality of life relates directly to quality of death.*

7. *With every loss there is a gain.*

8. *To contemplate one's death is to prepare for one's death.*

9. *Love transcends the fear of death as its reality lives on without the body.*

10. *Love is eternal, changeless, timeless and without form.*

THE PRINCIPLE'S MESSAGE

I was four years old when my Uncle Paul committed suicide. I can still vividly recall how intrigued I was by all the activity. I sensed a major life drama was occurring and that my parents tried to protect me and my brother from participating in it. The truth was I was not upset knowing that Uncle Paul was quietly lying in a casket in our living room. With great curiosity and wonder, I peeked around doors and watched the adults in action.

When I was five our neighbor lady was dying of cancer. I loved to visit her, always hitching my pretend wild bears, lions and monkeys to her shrubs before going in to talk with her. We spent hours together in joy and laughter. I remember it still.

It was about this time that I started organizing the children in the neighborhood to have funerals for all the dead animals we could find. My friends and I would put the animals in shoe boxes and bury them with flowers and a proper cross. I always played the role of funeral director and presiding minister. One day my adult cousin Martha stormed down the street and yelled at my mother, "Do you know Susan is having funerals? I won't have my children exposed to such things." My mother forbade me to collect any more dead animals and to have any more funerals. Suddenly death and I were no longer on friendly terms.

After that, even though I wanted to grieve whenever any relative, friend or pet died, I worked hard to be strong and swallow my tears. My family found it difficult to talk about death, even when my brother became seriously ill with cancer.

An event happened in my late twenties which opened the flood-gates of my swallowed tears and forced me to deal with my feelings about death. John Fitzgerald Kennedy and my ninety-year-old grandfather died on the same day. The combined grief I felt for our president's death and the death of my grandfather was overwhelming and had I not hung on to the stoic example of Jacqueline Kennedy I would have never been able to attend my grandfather's funeral. Out of rage and an attempt to punish him for the years of his sexually abusing me, I had not spoken to my grandfather for the last twenty years of his life. This family secret and my anger and guilt about it had adversely affected the quality of my life. The depth of my grief and the fact that it was almost uncontrollable told me that I couldn't put off confronting these issues any longer.

I decided to gently and slowly explore my feelings about life and death. First of all, I realized that I needed to heal my relationship with my grandfather. I started keeping a journal in which I wrote him letters and dialogued with him as though he were alive and able to speak with me. I did this until my rage and grief were released and I could truly forgive him and myself. Accompanying a physician friend, I spent hours in the emergency room and surgical room of a hospital. I visited graveyards until I felt totally comfortable in them. I worked with people with life-threatening illnesses. I began to talk about death to others until doing so felt natural again, just as it had when I was a small child. As I integrated death back into my life, I lost my hesitancy to live my life fully and meaningfully.

Some of my most cherished and loving moments have been with someone who is dying. When one feels comfortable with death, it is a sacred and joyous event. Without the fear of death, one can fully be in his true essence, love. Love and fear cannot coexist. When someone is dying, he wants to be with someone who is in his love essence in order to leave peacefully.

Fear of death equals fear of life. It is not the fear of death but the fear of living fully that impedes experiencing the joy of life. As one confronts the fear of living life fully, the fear of death goes away. Stephen Levine writes, "To become wholly born, whole beings, we must stop postponing life. To the degree we postpone life, we postpone death. We deny death and life in one fell swoop."[1]

One must fully accept the reality of his love essence in order for the fear of death to melt away. This is the love that is eternal and that passes from this reality into the next. This is the love that shines away the fear. To accept the reality of the presence of this love is the true task.

WHAT IS MY ATTITUDE?

Contemplate the following questions and write about your feelings in a journal.

1. Do I spend any time contemplating my own death? What is my reason for doing so or not doing so?

2. What are my feelings about my own death? Have I had any specific circumstances which have revealed these feelings to me?

3. What are my feelings about the death of those close to me?

4. What is my definition of death and dying?

5. What is the philosophical context in which I view death and have I made any preparations for my own death?

6. What are my experiences with death and how have they affected me?

7. How do I see the relationship between the quality of life and the quality of dying?

PRACTICING THE PRINCIPLE

Select the exercises that best facilitate and support your healing process, writing your responses in a journal. You may want to prerecord the visualization exercises.

1. When you can set aside about an hour of time, guide yourself through the following life-review imagery. This imagery is suggested by Carl and Stephanie Simonton and James Creighton in their book *Getting Well Again.*[2]

Sit in a comfortable position with nothing on your lap, feet flat on the floor and close your eyes. Rest in this comfortable state for a minute or two.

> Picture your physician telling you that your cancer has re-curred. (If you do not have cancer, imagine being told that you are dying.) Experience the feelings and thoughts you have in response to this information. Where do you go? Who do you call? What do you say? Take time to imagine the scene in detail.

> Now see yourself moving toward death. Experience whatever physical deterioration takes place. Bring into sharp focus all the details of the process of dying. Be aware of what you will lose by dying. Allow yourself several minutes to experience these feelings and to explore them in detail.

> See the people around you while you are on your deathbed. Visualize how they will respond to losing you. What are you

saying and feeling? Allow yourself ample time to see what is occurring. Imagine the moment of your death.

Attend your own funeral or memorial service. Who is there? What are they saying? What are people feeling? Again, allow yourself plenty of time.

See yourself dead. What happens to your consciousness? Let your consciousness go off to wherever you believe your consciousness goes after death. Stay there quietly for a few moments and experience that.

Then let your consciousness go out into the universe until you are in the presence of whatever you believe to be the source of the universe. While in that presence, review your life in detail. Take your time. What have you done that you are pleased with? What would you have done differently? What resentments did you have and do you still have? (Note: Try to review your life and ask yourself these questions no matter what you believe happens to your consciousness after death.)

You now have the opportunity to come back to earth in a new body and create a new plan for life. Would you pick the same parents or find new parents? What qualities would they have? Would you have any brothers and sisters? The same ones? What would your life's work be? What is essential for you to accomplish in your new life? What will be important to you? Think your new prospects over carefully.

Appreciate that the process of death and rebirth is continuous in your life. Every time you change your beliefs or feelings you go through a death and rebirth process. Now that you have experienced it in your mind's eye, you are conscious of this process of death and renewal in your life.

Now come back slowly and peacefully to the present and become fully alert.

After you have completed this imagery, you may want to write about your experience in your journal. As you repeat this imagery over time, you can identify the issues you have regarding the quality of your life and the status of their resolution.

2. Explore your beliefs about death by writing your own obituary. On a blank sheet of paper, begin a paragraph by writing the following sentence:

(your full name)_____ died today, ___(today's date)_____ in ___(location)_____.

Continue writing your own obituary in any way you wish, stating whatever you imagine or wish your obituary to say. Be creative. Write the kind of obituary you feel would truly convey the essence of your life.

Note any feelings or thoughts you have about this exercise. Read your obituary aloud and note any further feelings or thoughts.

3. Plan your funeral, addressing the following questions:

    a. Would I prefer to be buried or cremated, and if cremated, how should my family dispose of my ashes?

    b. If I am buried in a casket, what will it be made of? How do I want to be dressed?

    c. What kind of flowers do I want?

    d. Who will be my pallbearers?

    e. Where will the funeral be held?

    f. Is there any particular religious practice to be followed?

    g. Who will speak at my funeral? Do I have anything I would like him or her to say?

    h. Do I have any favorite music that I want played?

    i. Do I have any favorite poems or prose that I want read?

    j. What do I want inscribed on my tombstone?

4. Begin writing a Loving Will in which you note any feelings or

thoughts you have for significant persons in your life, to be read by them or to them after you have died. These are loving communications that you would like to express to each person, perhaps stating how you have valued having them in your life and how you wish them well.

5. Make two columns on a sheet of paper. On the left-hand side, write the various significant losses you have experienced in your life. These losses can relate to any stage of development from childhood through adulthood and can include any event in your life, positive or negative. On the right side, write what you have gained from that loss. For example:

<u>LOSS</u>	<u>GAIN</u>
Protection of home as a preschooler when I entered 1st grade	More exposure to other children
Moving from a small town to go to college	Broadening of life experiences
Divorce	Self-identity, emotional growth
Death of a child	Strength to confront fears of living and dying

6. Imagine you are lying on your deathbed. All significant people in your life come to see you, one at a time. Coming from your heart, you speak to each one. This is not a time to list your grievances but to express those communications which reflect the quality of your life and your desire to join with these people in a loving way. It is a time to let your mind sink into your heart, to let go of whatever binds you to being separate from them. Focus on the essentials of life; focus on its essence.

HAVE I HEALED MY ATTITUDE?

After practicing the above exercises, contemplate the following questions and write about your feelings in a journal.

1. What is my understanding now about the value and purpose of contemplating my own death?

2. What is the relationship between finishing business and the quality of life?

3. What is the value of allowing myself or another to move through the grieving process? Expand the meaning of the grieving process to include the many kinds of loss experienced in life, not just loss related to physical death.

4. What do I see as the most important factor in viewing death as fearful? As not fearful?

5. What does the phrase "love is eternal" mean to me? How does this statement relate to removing fear?

6. What does this thought mean to me, "I have a body but I am not a body"?

7. How am I specifically preparing for my own death?

APPLYING THE PRINCIPLE IN SERVICE

As an open and compassionate facilitator, you will experience your understanding of death and dying being challenged, expanded and deepened in a supportive relationship that centers around death and dying issues. Death, the dying process, grief and other forms of loss are all teachers and learning opportunities for your own emotional and spiritual growth.

Through witnessing someone else's process, you will become more aware of your own. Questions like "What would I do in that circumstance?" or "How would I respond to that news?" or "What would I do next as a way to approach the situation?" will come to mind. As you observe the person's deliberation process and see the dynamics of choice-making, you are asked to honor it all. When you fully honor the process of the dying person, you create a safe space for the person to explore his process to its highest level.

I have facilitated many people in their dying and death process and I have not had a duplicate experience. Each person has asked to be supported in his unique process, not wanting to be judged or made wrong. Some want only to be listened to, some want to learn how to meditate, some want to explore their emotional wounds, some want to do guided imagery. Some want the whole family to be involved, some want only the facilitator, some want to share their pain and anguish, some want to be surrounded by people, some want to be left alone. And, some want to experience their last days in joy. Your responsibility, as a facilitator, is to be sensitive to the process that the person wants and to support that choice. Rather than second-guessing, I have found it helpful to ask the person directly how he would like to be supported and to periodically reevaluate the supportive relationship. This checking-in approach is effective with adults and also with teenagers who ask for support after a suicide or death in their high schools.

As a facilitator for a dying person, you need to look carefully at your own personal views and understanding of death and the dying process. These views may be the same as or different from those of the person who is dying. You must ensure that your view is not intrusive on or judgemental of the view which the person holds. Sensitivity to others' view of death is necessary to be supportive and to serve their emotional and spiritual needs.

Usually everyone in the family needs someone who supports him or her personally when a member of the family is seriously ill or dying. You may or may not serve as a support person for more than one person in the family. The family should be clear about who you are specifically supporting.

Many points of view about death, including Eastern and Western spiritual traditions and the work of Elisabeth Kübler-Ross and Stephen Levine are necessary background for supporting the dying. Knowledge dispels the mystique of death and will help you to prepare for your own dying and death experiences and for your work with others.

If death is an issue for you, it is helpful to make a friend of it, get acquainted with it. Rather than viewing death as a failure, you can view it as an acknowledgement of a life fully lived. Death is the Oscar of success and completion of a step in the evolution of one's soul. Death can be viewed as a job well done this time around.

HOW AM I DOING?

Periodically assess your progress in applying this principle in service to others. Note your concerns, questions and feelings in a journal.

1. Am I continuing to educate myself about the physical, psychological and spiritual aspects of dying and death?

2. Am I open to the lessons to be learned from the person and family I am facilitating?

3. Am I increasingly more comfortable and willing to talk openly about death?

4. Am I improving my ability to be sensitive to how the person wishes to be supported in the dying process?

5. Am I better able to discern my issues with illness, dying and death and how they might differ from those of others?

6. Do I understand that with every loss there is a gain? Am I more aware of this concept when I am facilitating someone who is grieving losses other than those related to physical dying and death, such as losses related to divorce, job change, geographical relocation and so forth?

Chapter Sixteen

F or now we see through a glass, darkly;
but then face to face:
now I know in part;
but then shall I know even as also I am known.

I Corinthians, 13:12

Principle Twelve

WE CAN ALWAYS PERCEIVE OURSELVES AND OTHERS AS EITHER EXTENDING LOVE OR GIVING A CALL FOR HELP

BASIC TENETS

1. *In every situation, relationship or encounter, we are either extending love or giving a call for help.*

2. *Viewing another as always either extending love or giving a call for help asks that we look beyond appearances to the truth.*

3. *Calls for help come in many forms.*

4. *One asks for inner guidance in how to respond to a call for help.*

5. *Another person's call for help is a reminder of our own call for help.*

6. *Underlying all calls for help is a request to be reminded of our inner divinity.*

7. *Ourselves and others are not seen as victims and victimizers but as asking or calling for help.*

8. *The practice of this principle brings meaning and purpose to every human encounter and every human circumstance.*

9. *This principle is not about changing the behavior of another person but changing how we view that person's behavior.*

10. *A call for help is a call for love.*

THE PRINCIPLE'S MESSAGE

This principle requires complete integration of the other eleven. To practice it fully necessitates active application of all we have learned so far. This principle encompasses the whole of the definition of attitudinal healing.

Attitudinal healing is the ongoing process of healing the mind so that we can experience inner peace. This entails choosing a perception of the world that mirrors the inner state we want to create. Through the eyes of forgiveness we can see differently. We are in a constant state of choosing to perceive others as either extending love or asking for love. A request for love comes as an expression of fear – anger, guilt, resentment, helplessness and so on. As we practice inner peace we experience the natural inclination to share our inner state in service to the world. Our truest service is simply to see differently. All else flows from that.

This principle was made very real for me several years ago when I lived in San Francisco and was the head of a university medical center graduate training program and a clinic for children and adults with neurological learning and behavior disorders. I call what happened "The Mrs. W. Story."

From the moment that Mrs. W. first brought her daughter, Cynthia, to our department clinic for an evaluation, she seemed enveloped in a dark cloud of anger and resentment. Even during our initial assessment of her daughter's problem, Mrs. W. expressed great unhappiness with us. We did nothing "right." Nevertheless, after our evaluation, she decided to follow our recommendations and enrolled Cynthia in our clinic's treatment program.

During the entire time that Cynthia came to us, Mrs. W. persisted in expressing her displeasure with our services. If she called and asked for Miss Brown, who was the staff member in charge of Cynthia's treatment program, we knew Mrs. W. was again discontented. When she asked to speak to me as chairperson of the department, I knew she was particularly angry and distressed. I can still remember feeling my stomach churn when I was told Mrs. W. was on the line.

Our staff did its best to relate to Mrs. W. in a professional way. Mrs. W. continued her tirades and we continued to feel attacked by her. By responding in this way we were validating her fear. This way of relating went on for almost two years. We began to wonder why Mrs. W. even kept her daughter in our program.

One morning the staff and I decided that there had to be another way to work with Mrs. W. We decided to sit together and in meditation ask how we might better serve her and Cynthia.

As soon as I closed my eyes, I saw Mrs. W. standing in front of me, sending her usual barrage of complaints in my direction. Suddenly the words coming from Mrs. W. took the form of a cannonball, which started to propel itself towards me. Just as suddenly the cannonball was transformed into a cotton puffball. Then I saw myself lovingly hand Mrs. W. a beautiful rose, which she graciously accepted.

When the staff finished their meditations we discovered that we had each received essentially the same counsel. Our meditations reminded us to see Mrs. W.'s anger and complaints as a call for help, a call for love. By seeing her differently, we could respond by extending love to her in some way. We agreed to practice this visualization whenever we thought of or spoke to Mrs. W.

Soon after this Mrs. W. called and asked to speak to me. As we spoke on the phone, I visualized her angry words as a cannonball that transformed into a puffball and I saw myself handing her a beautiful red rose which she accepted. I continued this procedure every time she called and on some occasions I must have given her dozens and dozens of roses!

Six months after starting to use this visualization, I decided to leave San Francisco and move to Washington, D.C. I thought that, of all people, Mrs. W. would be the most delighted to hear the news. The day came when I was told Mrs. W. was on the phone. Her very first words to me were, "Oh, Dr. Trout, I hear that you are leaving. I am so sorry to hear that. The work that your department has done with my daughter has been wonderful." Caught by surprise, I responded, "Oh, Mrs. W., I had no idea you felt that way." She quickly interjected. "Well, you know, I have never felt so much love as I do in your hallway."

In the spirit of science, I asked, "Mrs. W., may I ask how long you have been feeling that way?" to which she immediately responded, "Oh, about the past six months."

I have told the Mrs. W. story in many speeches and workshops. Many people have now used this visualization in a variety of conflictual relationships. A particularly dramatic example was given to me by Rosemary, one of our Institute's facilitators and a graphic designer by profession. She shared the following:

> I had a very difficult meeting scheduled with a client. My associate and I were dreading this presentation. He had been demanding, unrelenting, disagreeable, and unappreciative. We were sure the designs we were bringing would meet with the kind of criticism we had come to expect from him.
>
> When this meeting started, I decided immediately to practice Principle 12 and so I mentally showered him with rose petals as my way of responding with love to his call for help.
>
> What happened was astonishing. He was appreciative, kind and very pleased with the work we had done. He expressed respect for the decisions we had made on the difficult parts of the project. And he was generous, insisting on paying us more for our work and urging us to bill him immediately, something which had never happened in my experience with him.
>
> I thought all of this was pretty spectacular. But what really impressed me was the fact that he subsequently sent my associate and me a dozen roses!

This principle is *not* about changing the behavior of another person or using the visualization in hopes of doing that. Rather, the principle is about changing how we view that person's behavior. It is about our inner attitude. There was no change in Mrs. W.'s behavior towards me or the staff during the six months. I probably would not have learned what effect my attitudinal change had had on her, if we had not spoken prior to my leaving San Francisco.

Taking the principle one more step, we need to see that another person's call for love is also our call for love. For example, Mrs. W.'s call for love reminded me of my own. As evidenced by my fearful reaction to her, I was not in a state of love myself when I related to her. Instead, I was responding from a place of defensiveness, fear and conflict. When I shifted my perception and changed my thoughts to loving ones, I could then extend love to Mrs. W., which is what she was really asking me to do.

The form of the love extended is revealed through inner guidance. Therefore, the extension of love takes different forms in different situations. In the two examples I have given thus far, the extension of love was in the form of mental imagery. In another situation, it might be to say something, or say nothing, to do something or do nothing.

Inner guidance calling for action is exemplified by this story: Catherine's mother was blissfully in love with a man whom her three adult children thought was swindling her of her life savings. For months the children and other relatives begged her to see what was happening, but she had a logical reason for all of the man's actions and refused to believe them. Catherine and her family sought advice from everyone. Legally they could do nothing. The situation became increasingly serious and the family felt desperately helpless.

Because of Catherine's knowledge of attitudinal healing, she and her siblings began to work with this principle, seeing the situation as a call for love for everyone concerned, including the swindler. Genuinely they asked for guidance and the solution came to them. Without the mother's knowledge, the siblings came from their homes all over the country, collected the necessary evidence and then surprised their mother one morning and lovingly showed it to her.

Catherine shared afterwards that this solution turned out to be a loving experience for herself, her siblings and her mother. Together, the siblings had sought assistance from the necessary banks and commercial people and also from the police. All were deeply touched by the love of these adult children for their mother. Imagine the impact on the mother to find that her adult children had come from all over the United States to rescue her! In the end, with the support of the family and a therapist, the mother confronted her denial of the situation and her healing process began. The man was arrested and he, too, has an opportunity to learn and heal.

This principle calls us to the active and ongoing practice of listening for guidance. It would be arrogant for us to think that we consciously know all the details about any given situation or person and thus know what is best. That part of us that is connected to the Divine Source *does know*. The more we communicate with this part of ourselves, the more compassionate and wise our service to others will be. We will also be more compassionate toward ourselves, have a greater awareness of our inner strength and have a clearer understanding of the unique purpose of our lives. In this way, we become our own best therapists.

Making this attitude a reality in your life takes time, practice and much willingness. The principle may sound simple, and it is. It is not, however, easy to practice. You will probably find that you do not automatically respond to a person's negative behavior or even your own as a call for help. With time you will begin to see your interactions with people differently and more often will ask the question, "What is the highest good for all in this situation?" and listen for an inner response.

WHAT IS MY ATTITUDE?

Contemplate the following questions and write about your feelings in a journal.

1. How do I react emotionally to a person whom I see as being unfair, intrusive, rejecting, depressed or angry?

2. Who in my daily life do I seem to react to in this way?

3. How strong is my motivation to really want to see these people as calling for help?

4. Am I aware of the many forms that a call for help can take? The many forms extending love can take?

5. Do I see any connection between a person's calling for love and my own?

6. How do I feel about the strength of my awareness of inner guidance?

7. In what way does asking within for guidance play a role in my life?

PRACTICING THE PRINCIPLE

Select the exercises that best facilitate and support your healing process, writing your responses in a journal. You may want to prerecord the visualization exercises.

1. Select a person in your life whose behavior you see as disruptive and negative towards you. On a blank sheet of paper and with colored pencils by your side, title the following three columns:

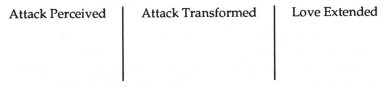

Attack Perceived	Attack Transformed	Love Extended

Now close your eyes and imagine the person standing in front of you. Imagine the person expressing himself to you in the way that you experience as negative. Allow yourself to see this negativity coming towards you in the form of a symbol. Do not imagine that the person is touching you in any way, but is instead sending this negativity towards you in the form of a symbolic representation of that negativity (as you recall, Mrs. W.'s expression of anger towards me took the form of a cannonball).

Now see this symbol transformed into an object that looks like the attack symbol but is so gentle it cannot hurt you (my cannonball became a cotton puffball). This symbol should be similar in shape, such as a knife becoming a feather, rocks becoming popcorn and so forth.

You now see yourself handing a symbol of love to this person and you imagine the person willingly accepting it. Again, this is to be a symbol of love, not a physical gesture or movement (a rose was my love symbol extended). The symbol of love needs to be one that both you and the person see as representing love in its highest form. Roses, lilies, lotuses, crystals and jewels are examples of this level of representation.

As you open your eyes, draw your images. Drawing them in color serves to imprint your desire for healing this relationship at an unconscious as well as at a conscious level.

Now affirm that whenever you think of this person or see him and experience attack, you will mentally use this imagery. There is no need to share this imagery with the person. Remember, it is your inner attitude that we are addressing here. Be aware of any changes you might have in your attitude towards this person.

2. Draw or find a picture that represents your form of extending love and place it in the environment in which you most often see or think about this person. You might even want to have the actual symbol in its physical form near you. For example, I have many pictures of roses and rose petals in my home and workplace.

3. Recall an incident in which you felt attacked by someone's behavior. In silence, return to that time and ask yourself this question, "What is the highest good for this person and myself? I am willing to be shown. I am willing to be taught. What am I to do or say?" In silence, allow the response to come to you. If it does not, trust that at some time during the day it will. Some of my most powerful answers have come to me later in the day or week, when I am seemingly thinking about something else or when I am brushing my teeth, taking a shower or driving the car.

4. Practice Exercise #3 when you are actually in a situation.

5. For one day, keep a log of the times you reacted to someone negatively or when someone reacted negatively to you. At the end of the day write next to each incident what help you sense the person and yourself were really asking for, i.e., to be understood, to be accepted, to be acknowledged and so forth.

6. Reread Chapter Thirteen. How does the principle, WE ARE STUDENTS AND TEACHERS TO EACH OTHER relate to the principle in this chapter?

HAVE I HEALED MY ATTITUDE?

After practicing the above exercises, contemplate the following questions and write about your feelings in a journal.

1. Am I experiencing more understanding of what it must be like to be in another person's shoes? Am I more sensitive to the life stories of others?

2. Am I more often seeing the other person's negative behavior as an expression of his own pain than as a deliberate action?

3. Do I have a deeper sense of humanity as one family, learning how to live and work together in this world?

4. Do I view negative situations between people as opportunities for a problem to be solved rather than further evidence that people are justified in taking victim-victimizer roles?

5. Am I more willing to see all interactions between myself and others as ones in which love is either being extended or being asked for?

6. Is it okay for me not to have expectations or see results from my application of this principle, particularly when I have been using a specific imagery?

7. Do I see how this principle relates to the principle, WE ARE STUDENTS AND TEACHERS TO EACH OTHER?

APPLYING THE PRINCIPLE IN SERVICE

This principle asks that you consistently view the person you are supporting as always either extending love or giving a call for help. This necessitates cultivating the discipline of asking within for guidance before responding to the person. Doing this assures you that the highest good is being served for that individual and for all others involved.

To feel assured that you are indeed receiving inner guidance in a situation calling for help, you need to develop and strengthen this connection within yourself. This is a lifelong learning process and necessitates commitment, discipline and discernment. There are several attitudes that foster access to one's Inner Voice:

1. Willingness to believe that within you there is a fount of wisdom and intuitive knowing that can become a source of higher

guidance in everyday life, for all "major" and "minor" decisions.

2. Willingness to make a commitment to enter into conscious dialogue with the Inner Voice and to trust It can answer quickly, surely and with love for everyone who will be touched in any way by the decision. One's Inner Voice is not necessarily an audible voice. Often, It is a fleeting thought, an intuitive feeling, an inner sense of "rightness."

3. Willingness to put in the necessary effort and discipline to learn from the Inner Voice, Who teaches you how to remove the blocks that stand between you and what you know. It takes repeated practice, prolonged patience and clear intention to refer all choices to the Inner Voice.

4. Willingness to give up a sense of worthlessness. This attitude asks that you be willing to say, "I know You, God, can communicate to me." God seeks to manifest through you and through all His children.

5. Willingness to be proven unfailingly reliable if God is to depend on you for any vital work. A helpful prayer in this regard is: "God, You can depend on me. I will listen to You and apply the knowledge I have received in my daily life. I will pay attention to my own rhythm of unfoldment and honor my own pace and way."

6. Willingness to listen to no other voice. The very fact we consciously and deliberately address ourselves to the Inner Voice has the result of blocking many of the lower voices. I, in isolation, do not know how to judge what is best for me or for another. If I decide to heed the Inner Voice sometimes and not others, I am placing an ego-self censor above that Voice.

7. Willingness to see differently, to perceive myself and others as One, to join others in defenseless bonding. We are not separate – we are One.

You will know you are truly "hearing" your Inner Voice if, as you follow it, you begin to experience more and more inner peace and if others spontaneously tell you that you seem more peaceful. You will also begin to experience less conflict in the world and have a greater awareness of your shared humanity. You will gradually experience less separation from others and from your inner divinity. In essence, you will have a greater awareness of the presence of equanimity throughout your day and in your response to situations and events.

HOW AM I DOING?

Periodically assess your progress in applying this principle in service to others. Note your concerns, questions and feelings in a journal.

1. Am I more consistently viewing the other person as either extending love or calling for help?

2. Have I become more aware of the range of forms that a call for help can take?

3. Am I more readily able to see in what ways the other person's call for help is my call for help?

4. Am I aware of extending love when I am in a supportive situation?

5. Do I more quickly and automatically ask for inner guidance when in a situation calling for help?

6. Am I feeling more confident that it is my Inner Voice I am hearing and not my ego-self?

7. Has asking for guidance become a more natural way of relating with the person I am supporting?

EPILOGUE

The train was waiting in the Moscow station, ready to take our group of seventy-eight Americans through the Soviet countryside to Helsinki, Finland. It was May, 1985, and we had just spent two weeks on a peace mission to the Soviet Union. Contrary to its intent, the trip had proven to be far from a peaceful experience for me. Instead, it had been a time of great emotional and spiritual upheaval.

As I waited in my Pullman compartment for the train to prepare for departure, I felt trapped in feelings of intense separation and alienation from my fellow Americans. From the outset I had felt separated in purpose and style from them and had quickly fallen into an abyss of emotional despair, feeling judged, compared and rejected. This feeling of alienation had become so intense by the end of our two weeks together that on the day of our departure, I sat in my compartment in a state of total anguish and fear. I was literally trapped in this pain. I knew I needed help to move out of this mental state. I desperately began to pray to God for help.

As I began praying, I heard a gentle knock at the door. A young man announced simply that the Indian Swami who was one of the people on the peace mission wanted to see me. From a distance I had observed his gentle nature and the way he seemed to take care of everyone; but, I had not met him.

When I was brought to the Swami, he greeted me by holding up a list of the names of the Americans and saying, "Susan Trout, I have met everyone on this trip but you. I had been really looking forward to meeting you – you have a lot of interesting information about who you are beside your name. Where have you been hiding? Who are you afraid of?"

To my surprise, I answered, "I'm afraid of you!" In that same instant it seemed to me the Swami became the size of my thumb and leapt into my heart! I literally felt the hand of God reach out and grasp the hand I had extended in my call for help. God in the form of the Swami had pulled me out of the quicksand of my fear of separation to safety. The gap had been bridged, the depth of the pain unearthed. In that moment, any doubt I had about the existence of or my connection with a Divine Source disappeared.

I am often reminded of my Soviet experience as I participate with others in their healing processes. Whenever a person in emotional pain takes the first and most essential step of genuinely asking God for help, help *does* come. The way it comes may be subtle or dramatic; but, it is always uniquely appropriate for the person asking for help. Grace seems to enter the person's life and his perceptions about self, relationships, events and situations begin to shift dramatically and move toward wholeness.

As I look back on my life I perceive my life experiences very differently from the way I viewed them originally. Now I clearly see the gifts of the events in my life and the gifts of my suffering – the gift of inner freedom, the gift of healing, the gift of trust, the gift of loving myself enough to accept the support of others and to extend it in return, the gift of the dynamic, joyous, living and creative reality called inner peace. It is as though I have walked through my pain to the other side of it, to the place where I have found the real me, the me that knows she is unconditionally loved and knows that she can serve from a place of unconditional acceptance. As I look forward, I see many experiences waiting. Some of them may be painful; but, I now know I can walk through them and choose to see them differently.

While writing this epilogue, I had another dream. I knew it was a final dream, an "amen" to bring this book to completion.

> *"Support is having a loving manner with another,"* a man says as he passes by and nods to me. His nod speaks of great gentleness and wisdom. His eyes communicate unconditional acceptance, his manner is nonintrusive. The tone of his voice alone expresses the sacredness of his message. What the man says and the manner in which he says it are in harmony; his mind and his heart are in alignment. He personifies the deep meaning of his words – we support others solely by having a *loving manner*.

In honor of your healing process and your unique expression of service to others, I acknowledge and support you, the reader. I wish you well. I say amen and thank you for the time we have been together through this book, knowing that we have truly shared a change in vision and a commitment to see differently.

NOTES

INTRODUCTION   (Pages 23-26)

1. *A Course in Miracles* (Tiburon, CA: Foundation for Inner Peace, 1976).
2. Kenneth Wapnick, *Absence From Felicity* (Roscoe, NY: "A Course in Miracles" Foundation, 1990). Robert Skutch, *Journey Without Distance* (Berkeley: Celestial Arts Publishing Co., 1984).
3. Carlos Castaneda, *The Teachings of Don Juan: A Yaqui Way of Knowledge* (New York: Simon & Schuster, Inc., 1974). p. 107. Originally published in 1968.

PART ONE: ATTITUDINAL HEALING

CHAPTER ONE: PHILOSOPHICAL FOUNDATIONS (Pages 29-34)

1. *A Course in Miracles*, op. cit., p. 572.
2. W. H. Murray, Scottish Himalayan Expedition. Unable to locate original source.

CHAPTER TWO: THE TWO TENETS (Pages 35-39)

1. Fyodor Dostoyevsky, *The Brothers Karamazov*, translated by Andrew H. MacAndrew (New York: Bantam Books, Inc., 1981), biographical page.

CHAPTER THREE: THE HEALING PROCESS (Pages 41-52)

1. Viktor E. Frankl, *Man's Search for Meaning* (New York: Simon & Schuster, Inc., 1984), pp. 86-87.
2. Ibid., p. 172.

3. Leo Tolstoy, *A Confession, The Gospel in Brief, What I Believe* (London: Oxford University Press, 1951), pp. 15-19.
4. Paraphrased from the readings of Edgar Cayce, The Edgar Cayce Foundation, Virginia Beach, VA.
5. Piero Ferrucci, *What We May Be* (Los Angeles: Jeremy P. Tarcher, Inc., 1982), p. 65.
6. Ram Dass and Paul Gorman, *How Can I Help?* (New York: Alfred A. Knopf, Inc., 1985), p. 99.

CHAPTER FOUR: BEING OF SERVICE (Pages 53-68)

1. *Holy Bible,* I Kings, 10:8
2. Ibid., I Kings 12: 9
3. Ibid., I Kings 2:3
4. Joseph Chilton Pearce, *The Magical Child* (New York: E. P. Dutton, 1977); see also *Magical Child Matures* (New York: E. P. Dutton, 1985). Alice Miller, *The Drama of the Gifted Child* (New York: Basic Books, Inc., 1981); see also *For Your Own Good* (New York: Farrar, Straus & Giroux, Inc., 1983); *Pictures of a Childhood* (New York: Farrar, Straus & Giroux, Inc., 1986); and *Thou Shalt Not Be Aware: Society's Betray of the Child* (New York: Farrar, Straus & Giroux, Inc., 1986).
5. Brother Lawrence of the Resurrection, *The Practice of the Presence of God* (New York: Paulist Press, 1978), p. 4.
6. See Peace Pilgrim, *Peace Pilgrim* (Santa Fe: Ocean Tree Press, 1982).
7. Scott Peck, *The Road Less Traveled* (New York: Simon and Schuster, Inc., 1978), p. 81.
8. Ferrucci, *What We May Be,* op. cit., p. 184.
9. These guidelines are adapted from those created by the Center for Attitudinal Healing, Tiburon, California.
10. Ann Landers, *The Washington Post* (25 December 1988).
11. Theodore Rosak, *Person/Planet: The Creative Disintegration of Industrial Society* (Garden City, NY: Anchor Press/Doubleday, 1978), p. xv.

PART TWO: THE TWELVE PRINCIPLES

CHAPTER FIVE: PRINCIPLE 1 - THE ESSENCE OF OUR BEING IS LOVE (Pages 73-82)

1. *Webster's Ninth New Collegiate Dictionary* (Springfield, Mass.: Merriam-Webster, Inc., 1988), p. 425.
2. Dostoyevsky, *The Brothers Karamazov,* op. cit., pp. 385-386.

3. See Kenneth Wapnick, *Forgiveness and Jesus* (New York: Coleman Publishing, Inc., 1983), pp. 2-3.
4. Stephen Levine, *A Gradual Awakening* (New York: Doubleday & Co., 1979), p. 94.
5. Joseph Campbell and Bill Moyers, *The Power of Myth* (New York: Doubleday & Co., 1988), p. 3.

CHAPTER SIX: PRINCIPLE 2 - HEALTH IS INNER PEACE. HEALING IS LETTING GO OF FEAR (Pages 85-100)

1. Bernie Siegel, *Love, Medicine and Miracles* (New York: Harper & Row, Publishers, 1986).
2. Mary Craig, *Spark from Heaven* (Notre Dame, IN: Ave Maria Press, 1988), pp. 162-163.
3. Ferrucci, *What We May Be*, op. cit., p. 55.
4. The original form of this exercise can be found in Roberto Assagioli's *The Act of Will* (New York: Penguin Books, 1974), pp. 214-216.
5. Lisa Mighetto, *Muir Among the Animals* (San Francisco: Sierra Club Books, 1986), p. 93.
6. Ibid., xviii.

CHAPTER SEVEN: PRINCIPLE 3 - GIVING AND RECEIVING ARE THE SAME (Pages 103-112)

1. L. Jesse Lemisch, *Benjamin Franklin: The Autobiography and Other Writings* (New York: NAL Penguin, 1961), pp. 94-98.
2. Edward LeJoly, *Mother Teresa of Calcutta* (San Francisco: Harper & Row, Publishers, 1983).
3. See Brother Lawrence, *The Practice of the Presence of God*, op. cit.; Peace Pilgrim, *Peace Pilgrim*, op cit.; and Julien Green, *God's Fool: The Life and Times of St. Francis of Assisi*. Translated by Peter Heinegg. (San Francisco: Harper & Row, Publishers, 1983).

CHAPTER EIGHT: PRINCIPLE 4 - WE CAN LET GO OF THE PAST AND OF THE FUTURE (Pages 115-126)

1. Helen Mallicoat, *My Name is I Am*. Unable to locate original source.
2. Miller, *For Your Own Good* , op. cit., p. xv.
3. Charles Whitfield, *Healing the Child Within* (Deerfield Beach, FL: Health Communications, 1987), p. 1.
4. Miller, *For Your Own Good*, op. cit., p. xi.

CHAPTER NINE: PRINCIPLE 5 - NOW IS THE ONLY TIME THERE IS AND EACH INSTANT IS FOR GIVING (Pages 129-140)

1. Joel S. Goldsmith, *Living Now* (Secaucus, NJ: Citadel Press, 1965), p. 60.
2. Ibid., p. 6.
3. Ibid., back cover
4. Levine, *Who Dies? An Investigation of Conscious Living and Conscious Dying.* (New York: Doubleday & Co., 1982), p. 202.
5. Madeleine L'Engle, *The Wind in the Door* (New York: Dell Publishing Co., Inc., 1962), p. 148.
6. Louis Savary and Patricia Berne, "Kything," *New Realities Magazine* (July/August 1989), pp. 33-46.

CHAPTER TEN: PRINCIPLE 6 - WE CAN LEARN TO LOVE OUR-SELVES AND OTHERS BY FORGIVING RATHER THAN JUDGING (Pages 143-153)

1. Geir Kjetsaa, *Fyodor Dostoyevsky: A Writer's Life* (New York: Fawcett Columbine, 1987), pp. 127, 106-107.
2. Lynn Minton, *The Washington Post.* (1 May 1988).
3. Ruth Carter Stapleton, *The Experience of Inner Healing* (Waco, TX: Word Books, 1977), pp. 62-63.
4. Levine, *Who Dies?* op. cit., p. 73.

CHAPTER ELEVEN: PRINCIPLE 7 - WE CAN BE LOVE-FINDERS RATHER THAN FAULT-FINDERS (Pages 157-166)

1. Roy Pinyoun, *Greener Pastures* (Raleigh, NC: Edwards & Broughton, 1977), pp. 51-52.

CHAPTER TWELVE: PRINCIPLE 8 - WE CAN CHOOSE AND DIRECT OURSELVES TO BE PEACEFUL INSIDE REGARDLESS OF WHAT IS HAPPENING OUTSIDE (Pages 169-180)

1. James Allen, *As A Man Thinketh* (Marina del Rey, CA: DeVorss & Co.), pp. 65-66.

CHAPTER THIRTEEN: PRINCIPLE 9 - WE ARE STUDENTS AND TEACHERS TO EACH OTHER (Pages 183-195)

1. Carl G. Jung. *Synchronicity: An Acausal Connecting Principle* (Princeton, NJ: Bollingen, 1973).

2. Jean Shinoda Bolen, *The Tao of Psychology* (San Francisco: Harper & Row, Publishers, 1979), pp. 23-24.
3. Levine, *Who Dies?* op. cit., p. 80.

CHAPTER FOURTEEN: PRINCIPLE 10 - WE CAN FOCUS ON THE WHOLE OF LIFE RATHER THAN THE FRAGMENTS (Pages 199-214)

1. Robert Johnson, *Ecstasy: Understanding the Psychology of Joy* (San Francisco: Harper & Row, Publishers, 1987), p. vii.

CHAPTER FIFTEEN: PRINCIPLE 11 - SINCE LOVE IS ETERNAL, DEATH NEED NOT BE VIEWED AS FEARFUL (Pages 217-226)

1. Levine, *Who Dies?* op. cit., p. 9.
2. O. Carl Simonton, Stephanie Matthews-Simonton and James Creighton, *Getting Well Again* (Los Angeles: Jeremy Tarcher, 1978), pp. 226-227.

BIBLIOGRAPHY

Achterberg, Jeanne. *Imagery in Healing: Shamanism and Modern Medicine.* Boston: Shambhala Publications, 1985.

Adair, Margo. *Working Inside Out: Tools for Change.* Berkeley: Wingbow Press, 1984.

Allen, James. *As A Man Thinketh.* Marina del Rey, CA: DeVorss & Co., n.d.

Andrews, Lewis. *To Thine Own Self Be True.* Garden City, NY: Anchor Press/Doubleday, 1987.

Assagioli, Roberto. *Psychosynthesis.* New York: Penguin Books, Inc., 1965.

_____ . *The Act of Will.* New York: Penguin Books, Inc., 1974.

Bass, Ellen and Laura Davis. *The Courage to Heal.* New York: Harper & Row, Publishers, 1988.

Blofeld, John. *Bodhisattva of Compassion: The Mystical Tradition of Kuan Yin.* Boston: Shambhala Publications, 1988.

Bolen, Jean Shinoda. *The Tao of Psychology.* San Francisco: Harper & Row, Publishers, 1979.

Bradshaw, John. *The Family: A Revolutionary Way of Self Discovery.* Deerfield Beach, FL: Health Communications, Inc., 1988.

Brallier, Lynn. *Transition and Transformation: Successfully Managing Stress.* Los Altos, CA: National Nursing Review, 1982.

Brandon, David. *Zen in the Art of Helping.* London: Unwin Brothers, 1976.

Campbell, Joseph, and Bill Moyers. *The Power of Myth.* New York: Doubleday & Co., Inc., 1988.

Campbell, Susan. *The Couple's Journey: Intimacy as a Path to Wholeness.* San Luis Obispo, CA: Impact Publishers, Inc., 1980.

Carlson, Richard, and Benjamin Shield. *Healers on Healing.* Los Angeles: Jeremy P. Tarcher, Inc., 1989.

Castaneda, Carlos. *The Teachings of Don Juan: A Yaqui Way of Knowledge.* New York: Simon & Schuster, Inc., 1974.

Cooper, J. C. *An Illustrated Encyclopedia of Traditional Symbols.* London: Thames & Hudson, 1978.

A Course in Miracles. Tiburon, CA: Foundation for Inner Peace, 1976.

Cousins, Norman. *Anatomy of an Illness as Perceived by the Patient.* New York: W. W. Norton & Co., 1979.

Craig, Mary. *Spark from Heaven.* Notre Dame, IN: Ave Maria Press, 1988.

Dass, Ram, and Paul Gorman. *How Can I Help?* New York: Alfred A. Knopf, Inc., 1985.

Delaney, Gayle. *Living Your Dreams.* New York: Harper & Row, Publishers, 1979.

Dostoevesky, Fyodor. *The Brothers Karamozov.* Translated by Andrew H. MacAndrew. New York: Bantam Books, Inc., 1981.

E., Stephanie. *Shamed Faced.* Center City, MN: Hazelden Foundation, 1986.

Ferrucci, Piero. *What We May Be.* Los Angeles: Jeremy P. Tarcher, Inc., 1982.

Fossum, Merle, and Marilyn Mason. *Facing Shame.* New York: W. W. Norton & Co., 1986.

Frankl, Viktor E. *Man's Search for Meaning.* New York: Simon & Schuster, Inc., 1984.

Furth, Gregg. *The Secret World of Drawings.* Boston: Sigo Press, 1988.

Goldsmith, Joel S. *Living Now.* Secaucus, NJ: Citadel Press, 1965.

Green, Julien. *God's Fool: The Life and Times of St. Francis of Assisi.* Translated by Peter Heinegg. San Francisco: Harper & Row, Publishers, 1983.

Hammarskjold, Dag. *Markings.* London: Faber & Faber, Ltd., 1966.

Hardy, Jean. *A Psychology with A Soul: Psychosynthesis in Evolutionary Context.* New York: Routledge & Kegan Paul, 1987.

The Impersonal Life. San Gabriel, CA: C. A. Willing, Publisher, 1975.

James, Walene. *Handbook for Educating in the New Age.* Virginia Beach, VA: A. R. E. Press, 1977.

Jampolsky, Gerald. *Love is Letting Go of Fear.* Berkeley: Celestial Arts Publishing Co., 1979.

_____ . *Teach Only Love: The Seven Principles of Attitudinal Healing.* New York: Bantam Books, Inc., 1983.

Johnson, Robert. *Ecstasy: Understanding the Psychology of Joy.* San Francisco: Harper & Row, Publishers, 1987.

Jung, Carl G. *Synchronicity: An Acausal Connecting Principle.* Princeton, NJ: Bollingen Paperback Edition, 1973.

Kjetsaa, Geir. *Fyodor Dostoevsky: A Writer's Life.* New York: Fawcett Columbine, 1987.

Kübler-Ross, Elisabeth. *On Children and Death.* New York: Macmillan Publishing Co., Inc., 1983.

Lawrence of the Resurrection, Brother. *The Practice of the Presence of God.* New York: Paulist Press, 1978.

LeJoly, Edward. *Mother Teresa of Calcutta.* San Francisco: Harper & Row, Publishers, 1983.

Lemisch, L. Jesse. *Benjamin Franklin: The Autobiography and Other Writings.* New York: NAL Penguin, 1961.

L'Engle, Madeleine. *The Wind in the Door.* New York: Dell Publishing Co., Inc., 1962.

_____ . *A Ring of Endless Light.* New York: Dell Publishing Co., Inc., 1982.

Levine, Stephen. *A Gradual Awakening.* New York: Doubleday & Co., Inc., 1979.

_____ . *Who Dies? An Investigation of Conscious Living and Conscious Dying.* New York: Doubleday & Co., Inc., 1982.

Miller, Alice. *The Drama of the Gifted Child.* New York: Basic Books, Inc., 1981.

_____ . *For Your Own Good.* New York: Farrar, Straus & Giroux, Inc., 1983.

_____ . *Pictures of a Childhood.* New York: Farrar, Straus & Giroux, Inc., 1986.

_____ . *Thou Shalt Not Be Aware: Society's Betrayal of the Child.* New York: Farrar, Straus & Giroux, Inc., 1986.

Mighetto, Lisa. *Muir Among the Animals.* San Francisco: Sierra Club Books, 1986.

Morningstar, Rose. *A Course in Crystals: Lessons in Personal Transformation and Global Healing.* New York: Harper & Row, Publishers, 1989.

Myrick, Robert, and Tom Erney. *Youth Helping Youth: A Handbook for Training Peer Facilitators.* Minneapolis: Educational Media Corp., 1979.

_____ . *Caring and Sharing: Becoming a Peer Facilitator.* Minneapolis: Educational Media Corp., 1978.

Muktananda, Swami. *Reflections of the Self.* South Fallsburg, NY: SYDA Foundation, 1980.

Peace Pilgrim. *Peace Pilgrim.* Santa Fe: Ocean Tree Press, 1982.

Pearce, Joseph Chilton. *The Magical Child.* New York: E. P. Dutton, 1977.

_____ . *Magical Child Matures.* New York: E. P. Dutton, 1985.

Peck, Scott. *The Road Less Traveled.* New York: Simon & Schuster, Inc., 1978.

Pinyoun, Roy. *Greener Pastures.* Raleigh, NC: Edwards & Broughton, 1977.

Progoff, Ira. *At a Journal Workshop.* New York: Dialogue House Library, 1975.

_____ . *The Well and the Cathedral: An Entrance Meditation.* New York: Dialogue House Library, 1972.

_____ . *The White Robed Monk.* New York: Dialogue House Library, 1972.

Roszak, Theodore. *Person/Planet: The Creative Disintegration of Industrial Society.* Garden City, NY: Anchor Press/Doubleday, 1978.

Sanford, John. *Healing and Wholeness.* New York: Paulist Press, 1977.

Savary, Louis, and Patricia Berne. "Kything." *New Realities Magazine,* July/August, 1989.

Schwarz, Jack. *Human Energy Systems.* New York: E. P. Dutton, 1980.

Siegel, Bernie. *Love, Medicine and Miracles.* Harper & Row, Publishers, 1986.

Simonton, O. Carl, Stephanie Matthews-Simonton, and James Creighton. *Getting Well Again.* Los Angeles: Jeremy P. Tarcher, Inc., 1978.

Skutch, Robert. *Journey Without Distance.* Berkeley: Celestial Arts Publishing Co., 1984.

Stapleton, Ruth Carter. *The Experience of Inner Healing.* Waco, TX: Word Books, 1977.

Stone, Hal, and Sidra Winkelman. *Embracing Each Other: Relationship as Teacher, Healer and Guide.* San Rafael, CA: New World Library, 1989.

_____ . *Embracing Ourselves: The Voice Dialogue Manual.* San Rafael, CA: New World Library, 1989.

Tanner, Wilda. *The Mystical Magical Marvelous World of Dreams.* Tahlequah, OK: Sparrow Hawk Press, 1988.

Tatelbaum, Judy. *The Courage To Grieve.* New York: Harper & Row, Publishers, 1980.

Tolstoy, Leo. *A Confession, The Gospel in Brief, What I Believe.* London: Oxford University Press, 1951.

Trout, Susan. *A Basic Facilitator Training Course in Attitudinal Healing: Manual for Group Leaders. Revised Edition.* Washington D. C.: Three Roses Press, 1990.

Verny, Thomas, with John Kelly. *The Secret Life of the Unborn Child.* New York: Dell Publishing Co., Inc., 1981.

Wapnick, Kenneth. *Forgiveness and Jesus.* New York: Coleman Publishing, Inc., 1983.

_____ . *Absence from Felicity.* Roscoe, NY: "A Course in Miracles" Foundation, 1990.

Welch, John. *Spiritual Pilgrims: Carl Jung and Teresa of Avila.* New York: Paulist Press, 1982.

White, John. *A Practical Guide to Death and Dying.* Wheaton, IL: Theosophical Publishing House, 1980.

Whitfield, Charles. *Healing the Child Within.* Deerfield Beach, FL: Health Communications, Inc., 1987.

Whitmore, Diana. *Psychosynthesis in Education.* Rochester, VT: Destiny Books, 1986.

Wilber, Ken. *No Boundary: Eastern and Western Approaches to Personal Growth.* Boulder: Shambhala Publications, 1979.

COPYRIGHT
ACKNOWLEDGEMENTS

ABOUT THE AUTHOR

Susan S. Trout, Ph.D., is Executive Director of the Institute for Attitudinal Studies in Alexandria, VA. Within the philosophical framework of attitudinal studies, Dr. Trout coordinates and develops support and study programs, trains group leaders, leads workshops in personal growth, trains individuals to be facilitators for those having physical, emotional or spiritual health needs and develops research projects in mind-body-spirit disciplines.

Prior to becoming co-founder and Executive Director of the Institute, Dr. Trout spent fourteen years as a professor, chairperson and researcher at the University of the Pacific Medical Center, San Francisco. She holds graduate degrees from Stanford and Northwestern Universities in psychoneurology and communication disorders. She is the author of several professional articles and has authored training manuals in attitudinal studies for adults and adolescents.

ABOUT THE INSTITUTE FOR ATTITUDINAL STUDIES

P. O. Box 19222
Alexandria, VA 22320
703-706-5333

As a volunteer, nonprofit, educational and non-sectarian spiritual organization, the Institute for Attitudinal Studies offers service, training, research and publishing programs dedicated to personal growth and community service within the philosophical framework of attitudinal studies. The core processes of attitudinal studies are personal healing, service, facilitation, communication, conflict resolution, leadership and organizational design. Contributing disciplines include psychosynthesis, the enneagram, attitudinal healing, depth psychology, dream psychology, death and dying, energy work, metaphysics, and western and eastern spiritual thought.

Support groups, facilitation and conflict resolution services, study groups, courses and workshops are offered by the Institute that support the emotional and spiritual well-being of people of all ages in a wide variety of life circumstances.

Extensive training programs prepare adults and high school students to be facilitators and mediators and prepare group leaders to lead these trainings. Trainings for individuals and organizations are also offered in leadership, organizational design, team building, group process and conflict resolution.

Research projects evaluate the effectiveness of the Institute's trainings, prepare materials on leadership and organizational models and study the dynamics of the healing process and service.

INDEX

Abandonment, 99, 204
Absence from Felicity, 24
Abundance, 108, 131
Abuse, 29, 116, 205; physical, 47; psychological, 47, 152; sexual, 185, 192, 201, 213, 218; spiritual, 152; substance, 25, 60, 74, 202
Abusive family, 88
Acceptance, 87, 106, 111, 165, 172; of illness, 87; of self, 165
Accountable: for our perceptions, 116; for our projections, 121, 187
Acknowledgement, 110, 111, 112, 116, 117, 118, 124, 131, 132, 137, 144, 159, 160; *exercise*, 206
Acknowledging healing and growth, 43, 51-52; *exercise*, 162; love-finds, 158; progress, 99; what was given and received, 110
Acquiring life experiences, 212
Action, selfless, 133
Acupuncture, 23
Addiction, 60, 116, 152, 185, 201, 205, 213; as negative side of spiritual seeking, 205; of self-doubt, 74
Adult self who heals/reparents inner child, 117
Advice, 59, 61, 62, 63, 65
Affirmations, 18, 97; about love-finds, 163; disidentification, 95-96; fears and *(exercise)*, 95; of wholeness *(exercise)*, 207
Agreements, 164
Alaska, 97
Alcohol, 201

Alcoholic, 189
Alcoholics Anonymous, 89
Alexei (in *Brothers Karamazov*), 74-75
Alignment of heart and mind, 119-120, 124, 126, 131, 133, 136
Aliveness, 81
Allen, James, 178
Alone, spending time, 62
Allowing the process to unfold, 43, 48-51
Amen, 242, 243
"Angel" in audience, 172
Anger, 29, 32, 49, 62, 75, 85, 194, 218, 230, 231, 234
Animals, healing effect of, 75
Answers, 59, 62
Anxiety, 116
Appearances: looking beyond, 73, 189, 206, 210, 229; seeing beyond, 199, 213, 214
Arabs, 172
Armstrong, Neil, 42
Assagioli, Roberto: disidentification exercise, 95-96
Assumptions, 31, 32-33, 99, 100, 125, 126, 164
Astronaut imagery *(exercise)*, 209-210
Astronauts, 200
Attachments, 200, 212
Attack, 164, 171, 172, 231; perceived and transformed *(exercise)*, 235-236
Attitudes, 17, 43; changing, 235-236 *(exercise)*; choosing, 170; negative, 73
Attitudinal change, 232
Attitudinal healing, 16, 23, 24-26, 29,

263

ORDERING INFORMATION

- Copies of *To See Differently* may be ordered directly from the Three Roses Press

Cost: $12.95

- Card sets are also available. These consist of fourteen cards, one for each principle of attitudinal healing, plus a card for the communication guidelines and one for the facilitator guidelines. Each principle card includes the tenets for that principle and questions for reflection.

Cost: $ 7.95

Please send me the following:

_____ copies of the book TO SEE DIFFERENTLY x $12.95 =	
_____ sets of ATTITUDINAL HEALING PRINCIPLES: A CARD SET x $ 7.95 =	
_____ copies of the Institute for Attitudinal Studies Newsletter x $ 1.50 =	

Postage & Handling: Domestic: $3.00 for the first item for each address; $1.00 for each additional item. Foreign: $3.00 for the first item for each address; $1.50 for each additional item.	Subtotal
Note: No postage or handling charge for the newsletter. **Method of Payment:** Please enclose check or money order payable to the THREE ROSES PRESS, in U.S. dollars. No C.O.D.'s. Outside the U.S., pay by International Postal Money Order in U.S. funds or in U.S. dollars	Shipping & Handling
drawn on U.S. banks only. **Bulk Orders:** Call for special book and card prices for volume orders: (703) 706-5333	TOTAL

Name _____

Shipping Address _____

_____

City _____ State _____ Zip Code _____

Telephone: Home _____ Office _____

Mail Orders to: **Three Roses Press**
                     P.O. Box 19222
                     Alexandria, VA 22320
                     Telephone: (703) 706-5333